The Uncertain Father

The Uncertain Father

Exploring Modern Fatherhood

Richard Seel

Gateway Books, Bath

First published in 1987
by GATEWAY BOOKS
19 Circus Place
Bath, BA1 2PW

Distributed in the USA by
SLAWSON COMMUNICATIONS
3719 Sixth Avenue
San Diego, CA 92183

Cover design & illustrations by Adrian Obertelli

Set in 10½ on 12pt Palatino
by Wordsmiths of London
Printed and bound by
Biddles of Guildford

British Library Cataloguing in Publication Data

Seel, Richard
    The uncertain father:
    exploring modern fatherhood
    1. Fathers
    I. Title
    306.8'742 HQ756
ISBN: 0.946551.26.X

Contents

To Shirley, Mark, Adam, & Rebecca
- who have shown me the joy of fatherhood,
and have dispelled my own uncertainties.

Acknowledgements

Writing is a lonely occupation, and self-confidence rapidly ebbs. At such times any spark of help or encouragement is eagerly accepted. I am particularly grateful to John, Andy, Chris, Ian, Stuart, Gary, Martin, Robert, Mick, Alistair, Jeff, Rob, David, Sid, and all the other men whose stories and experiences are told in these pages. Their willingness to share with me their experiences and expectations of fatherhood was crucial to the content and argument of the book.

I also want to thank the many women who showed an interest in the book and who spoke frankly of their feelings about parenthood. Many of my contacts were made as a result of my work with the National Childbirth Trust (NCT) whose magazine New Generation I was privileged to edit for the first three years of its life. I would not wish to commit the NCT to any of the opinions expressed in this book, but there is no doubt that I could not have written it without the invaluable help and encouragement I have received from many NCT members. I am also grateful to Dr Bill Hague, who helped me with the biological portions of chapters three and eleven - although of course he is not responsible for any errors.

Finally, and most importantly, I owe a special debt of gratitude to John Biggs, and to Judy and Tony Priest, who all spent many hours reading my turgid drafts and making detailed comments. Their help and support was invaluable and although they can accept no blame for any remaining inadequacies in the book, they must take much credit for any positive qualities it might have.

Richard Seel, October1986

1. What is a Father?

In English, the verb 'to mother' means to comfort, nurture, love. It implies a continuity of relationship, requiring effort and commitment over a period of time.

In English, the verb 'to father' means to sire, to be the producer of the spermatazoon which fertilizes the egg which becomes the child. It implies a single act requiring little effort and absolutely no commitment over a period of time.

I have been a father for thirteen years and I find it impossible to accept such a crude distinction between mothers and fathers. So do most other men I know. But it wasn't until a few years ago that circumstances led me to consider fatherhood more deeply; asking questions and thinking about it in ways which had never occurred to me before.

In the course of my work with the National Childbirth Trust, which is Britain's premier organization for antenatal education, breastfeeding counselling, and postnatal support, I discovered that many parents seem to be unsure about what it means to be a father today. They have a general agreement that the nature of fatherhood has changed over the course of the last generation, but no clear idea of the way a 'modern father' is supposed to behave.

I began to ask myself some questions: "What is the the father's role today?" "How is he different from his own father?" As I talked and read more, it became clear that there were many conflicts and contradictions lurking just below the surface. Everyone accepts that modern fathers are more involved with their children, but strangely, most of the research suggests that there has actually been little change in the amount of childcare work done by fathers. Today's men are certainly more involved in pregnancy and birth than the previous generation, but it is unclear whether this pattern continues as the babies grow up.

Mothers were ambivalent too. On the surface they seemed to welcome and encourage the changes. Indeed, it is often the mothers who are pushing their partners into involved fatherhood. But I also became aware of resentments and resistance, which were seldom openly articulated, but which came out more strongly as we talked.

Different styles and approaches to fatherhood became clear. Many men are uncertain about the best approach to adopt — and even less clear whether their personal circumstances will allow them to follow through with their chosen style. Old certainties seem to have disappeared — to be replaced with a bewildering freedom of choice; a freedom which often proves to be illusory when the new father tries to put it into practice.

I also began to realize that it wasn't just our ideas about the father's *role* which needed to be clarified. We are also beginning to change our ideas about the very definition of fatherhood itself. Higher divorce rates, and the fact that women are usually given custody of children, have led to a situation where many men no longer spend all their lives looking after one set of children. Instead they spend more time and attention with step-children than with their natural children.

The ties of biology are further weakened by practices such as artificial insemination by donor (AID). The husband of a woman who has AID almost invariably acts as father to the child, and since the fact of the artificial insemination is usually unknown to friends and neighbours he is treated just like any other father, even though he is not biologically related to the child.

I came to realize that here was another question which needs to be answered: "What is it that makes someone a father?" It turns out that different societies throughout the world have very different, and sometimes surprising, answers. But until we know just what it means to be a father it is hard to discover how a father ought to behave. The two questions are inevitably linked.

This book is the fruit of my attempt to explore some of the complexities of fatherhood. It is the result of a personal journey which has covered a lot of ground. In order to come to terms with the subject I have felt it necessary to adopt two very different perspectives. Sometimes I have relied on the results of academic research, especially in the fields of psychology, biology and anthropology. At other times I have found more enlightenment from my personal contacts with other parents and from accounts of their individual experiences.

And also, because I am a father and so part of the field of study, I have not hesitated to include my own experiences where they can help me to understand better. But there are no grand conclusions; it is very much 'work in progress'.

One thing which has struck me most forcibly is that there is now no obviously 'right' way to be a father. Sometimes a society expects a man to be active in the upbringing of his children; committed to their care. Sometimes he will be expected to spend most of his time doing other things; a distant figure rarely seen. There is no one pattern of fatherhood which has been universally accepted throughout history; there is no one pattern of fatherhood which is accepted throughout the world today.

There are some societies where there is a consensus about the proper way to father; in others there is no general agreement. We are now in the latter position: looking round for new ways to father, examining the old ways critically. Some people today — mainly women, it has to be admitted — are self-conscious about fatherhood. They want to talk about it, think about it, worry about it. Indeed the 'modern father' has become quite fashionable, especially in women's magazines! These now tell us of the 'new breed of father' who looks after the children while his wife works, and who has thrown aside all the trappings of traditional Victorian fatherhood. The implication is that all fathers should be like this — and that soon they will be.

There is an element of truth in these sensational and sentimental fantasies. Only one generation ago we did have a set of generally accepted rules. Now the values of this traditional fatherhood are being questioned and gradually overturned. In their place new definitions are slowly emerging. Perhaps in the future we will again enjoy the comfort of an accepted set of rules about fatherhood. But in the meantime we are in a state of flux, drawing both from the values of traditional fatherhood and also from some of the newer ideas.

This comes home to me most strongly when I give talks or run study days on parenting. I often use a questionnaire to get the discussion going, asking the participants to fill it in, not as a piece of scientific research but rather as an aid to thought and discussion. Many people find it rather infuriating — they don't like the way the questions are framed — but that too is part of the design, to help them consider more closely some aspects of parenting that they may take for granted. It is designed to find out what people think an ideal father or mother should be like, rather than to test their own experience or performance — although of course the two are closely connected.

How important are these to fatherhood?

(On a scale of 1 - 5; where 5 is very important, and 1 unimportant)

1) Good at mending things; from broken toys to blocked toilets

2) Being tender; able to wipe away tears and kiss it better

3) Playful; everything from rough and tumble to doll's tea parties

4) Keeping discipline; making sure children are obedient

5) Good provider; able to fork out for things they want

6) Good at housework; from cooking to dusting

7) Being cuddly; just for the pleasure of it

8) Ensuring that boys don't become too effeminate or girls too tomboyish

9) Tough; physically strong, not making a fuss about pain or discomfort

10) Able to take principle responsibility for child's welfare

11) Taking a pride in child's appearance and cleanliness

12) Clever; able to help with homework and TV quizzes

Now, in your own words, answer the final question, "What is the difference between a mother and a father?"

Both men and women have completed the forms, and I have also asked some women to score the same questions, but instead to relate their importance to motherhood. In this way I have been able to get some indication of what they think are the differences between motherhood and fatherhood. There are two main conclusions which come from the discussions and analysis of the forms.

Firstly, ideas about fatherhood *have* changed dramatically from the stereotype of the Victorian father with which most of us are familiar. Secondly, many people now see very little difference between the ideal mother and the ideal father.

This can be illustrated by looking at a few of the findings. For instance, take the three topics which the traditional father might have scored very low, and which are traditionally associated with motherhood: tenderness, housework, and cuddliness. Nearly all the men I spoke to said that 'being tender' is very important and three quarters of them felt the same way about 'being cuddly'. Interestingly, no-one was as keen on 'good at housework'; forty per cent of them scoring it low — in this respect at least things don't seem to have changed so much.

The same trend can be seen if we look at the things which the traditional father might think most important - such as 'being a good provider', 'keeping discipline', 'ensuring that the differences between males and females were properly observed'. Very few of the fathers thought that this latter role was at all relevant (one scored it as -10,000!), and most claimed that being a good provider was not now an important part of being a good father. Feelings about discipline were more mixed: equally divided as to whether discipline was crucial or irrelevant.

The stereotype of the traditional mother seems to have changed as well, although not so much. The biggest differences seem to be that women today don't see housework as a crucial part of mothering, and there is more emphasis on toughness, ability to mend things, and keeping discipline than one might have expected.

It was also very clear that many people did not want to make clear distinctions between male and female parents. This conclusion is backed up by the discussions and by the other comments people put on their forms. The following are typical of the answers people gave to the question, "What is the difference between a mother and a father":

> Little or none. Either should be able to turn their hand to all aspects of child care and homemaking should the need arise. (*mother*)

> Negligible in themselves. Different where they have been taught so. None of these things are vital/irrelevant — so being incapable of many of them does not make anyone a bad father/mother — especially if the one partner complements the other. (*father*)

> This depends so much on their personalities. I believe there should be a muddying of roles. Unsuccessful fathers are those who are always strong-willed and insist on macho boys, and girly girls. Unsuccessful mothers are those who do everything for their children and bring up boys and girls to believe this is

what wives should do. (*mother*)

Very few. Father marginally more good at mending things. (*father*)

Both are of prime importance to the child. Whoever is the main caretaker obviously has differences in role. These roles should be interchangeable with no adverse effects on the child, and this can be achieved. Mothers may be closer to baby whilst breastfeeding than fathers? (*mother*)

None essentially, each should complement the other. (*father*)

Once upon a time there were two separate stereotypes of father and mother, but now we have moved to a combined one which describes either. In this process, the stereotype of the mother has changed far less than that of the father. Those items which the traditional father might have scored highly are now scored very low. Those items which the traditional mother might have scored highly are still scored high.

We seem to have arrived at a position where fatherhood has become a sort of male motherhood! Although motherhood as a role has changed and evolved it is still recognizable, whereas fatherhood as a role has changed so much that for some parents it has almost been eliminated as a separate entity. What we are left with is *parenthood* — an activity which in theory can be undertaken by either men or women without distinction.

Amongst the parents I have spoken to the most common idea is that although there are no intrinsic differences between fathers and mothers, they should be complementary to each other in a particular relationship. It is tempting to conclude that the traditional values of very separate roles for fathers and mothers have been swept aside and replaced by this new ideology of sharing and co-operation. This is what many of the popular books and magazine articles suggest — but it is quite wrong.

For a start, several parents acknowledged that, although they wished that there were no differences, in practice it is still women who usually do more child care, and so are closer to their children. Women tend to stress the importance of men's working patterns as the key factor in distinguishing between mothers and fathers, while men are more likely to appeal to biology as the root of the differences:

Cultural: Mother, foreground — warmth, tenderness, continuities of home life. Father, background — provider, voice of discipline. Social: two halves of family team. Mother: routine, values for life, thoughts and opinions. Father: more time for play, creativity, experience outside the home. Mother: the home, family caring. Father: the world, work, etc. I think these are some 'differences', I don't mean to imply I agree with them! (*mother*)

Conventionally, the mother makes all main decisions on child's welfare — but this should change. Obviously main links in early days via breastfeeding — mother's greater opportunity for bonding. Mother having to handle shift of emphasis from partner to child; conventional father feeling left out. (New style father being equally involved and very understanding, gives and receives affection equally...) (*father*)

Mother carries baby antenatally. Mother generally has no choice but to take responsibility for child. Father generally has outside interest but also therefore has to cope with leaving child etc. Father is often excluded from day-time child activities, e.g. toddler group. If mother needs/wants to work she must find adequate care for child — also needs to cope with pressure about working instead of being home. Mother at home may be isolated. (*mother*).

Although the majority of the middle class committed parents I speak to are in favour of the 'new father', there are some who are still attached to traditional values. They believe that there are some natural differences between men and women and that these are reflected in different styles of parenthood:

Motherly	Fatherly
Ordinary	Able
Tender	Tireless
Helper	Helper
Effeminate	Ensuring
Responsive	Responsible
	(*expectant father*)

In any standard relationship, father is absent for a good two thirds of a child's day — mothers therefore have a better understanding of their own child's needs and temperament. On a personal level, while my husband loves our children and is perfectly capable of caring for them, he resents their presence if he has something 'better' to do. Mothers tend to be less self-centred through necessity. (*mother*)

Mother gains her authority over the children from the father. Father has ultimate responsibility for the education and upbringing of children (discipline, welfare, etc.) (*father*)

Fathers like to see children achieve, want their sons particularly to do as well as or better than themselves. Mothers provide the 'homely' atmosphere. More likely to show concern over minor illness. Differences very variable depending on cultural/geographical/social class backgrounds. (*female health worker*)

The ideals which the Victorian father epitomized have not vanished. It is simply that they are now being strongly challenged. We live in an era when different and apparently contradictory ideologies are being used at the same time. This may be a bit confusing as far as modern fatherhood is concerned, but it is not the first time it has happened with regard to parenthood. Charlie Lewis suggests that, at least since the 1920s, there has always been a belief that the current generation of parents were more involved with their children than their own parents were. Hand in hand with this has gone the feeling that the marriage patterns of the day had become more 'companionate'; less dependent on separate and highly differentiated roles for husband and wife, and with more emphasis on mutual affection and companionship. Although there may have been some real changes over the last thirty years, it also seems that these changes are not as radical as we sometimes think.

Some writers have suggested that cultures often have different sets of ideologies 'lying around' so that they can be used when they are needed. Sometimes the social and environmental conditions will favour the adoption of one set of ideals, sometimes another. But even when one ideology is dominant, the others will still be in the background; perhaps upheld only by a few eccentrics, until they are needed again.

An example of this was to be found in the prophets of ancient Israel. During times of peace and plenty they were largely ignored. Whatever the truth and importance of their message, they had little influence. The establishment, made up of the priests and royal court, led the people in a secular way of life. But when enemies threatened or the state collapsed, the people turned to the prophetic tradition to provide them with a sense of national identity and purpose. At such times the prophets became very powerful, almost national heroes, and their way was followed.[1]

I find this idea helpful when I try to come to terms with what is happening to fatherhood at present. We have, in our culture at the moment, some very different views of what fatherhood should be. Although there are people who subscribe enthusiastically to one type or another, most oscillate somewhere between the extremes. There are some who enjoy the freedom offered by the present situation. They are able to appeal to one or another extreme to justify their behaviour or to guide them along the path they think they ought to follow.

Sometimes this is done quite deliberately — almost cynically — but most are usually unaware of the way they give their allegiance to different ideologies in different circumstances. There are many others for whom the present uncertainty is distressing. They find life easier if they have obvious and accepted guidelines, and are often anxious and unsure of themselves when a role is not clearly defined. Most of us want to have out cake and eat it — we enjoy the freedom, but wish we could have the stability as well.

The relationship between people's ideals and the way they actually behave is not a simple one. Sometimes the ideology is fitted to the behaviour, as suggested above, but the opposite is also possible. For instance, Mormons believe that a father should adopt a very patriarchal position in the home. This is a matter of religious duty and belief. But a study carried out during the 1950s showed them to be affected by the general trend towards more power sharing between husband and wife.[2] The ideal of the all-powerful father was kept, but in practice he was now much more likely to take the opinions of the rest of the family into account before making decisions.

The lack of correspondence between ideals and behaviour is one of the reasons why it is so hard to answer questions like, "Are fathers *really* more involved now than they used to be?" Many men have adopted an ideology which maintains that a father *ought* to be involved with his children, but for one reason or another they actually do little more at home than the traditional father.

The wide range of attitudes towards fathering makes it almost impossible to generalize about the modern father. In an attempt to make some sense out of this diversity I have found it useful to look at fathers in two different ways: according to the amount of commitment they have to fatherhood, and according to the kind of fatherhood they think appropriate. This can be illustrated by looking at the extremes of each.

There seem to be two particularly important qualities connected with the *kind* of fathering a man adopts: one relates to the way authority is exercised within the home and the other to the amount of involvement in the home which the father ought to have. At the one extreme is the *traditional father*. He is the man who is still in thrall to the values of Victorian fatherhood. He may love his children deeply, but doesn't see any need to express his concern in practical childcare. Rather, his role is that of bread winner, ultimate authority, and stable foundation upon which the rest of the household is built. Despite many reports of his demise, the traditional father is still common and shows no sign of dying out as quickly as some people wish.

The *active father* has adopted the other ideological extreme from the traditional father. He wants to take genuine responsibility for the care of his children and gives his home life a higher priority than his work. He does not see his role as one of 'helping out'; rather that childcare tasks and decisions should be shared equally by parents. He sees no reason why men shouldn't parent just as well as women, and believes that some men make better parents than some women.

The other way of looking at fatherhood involves asking how *committed* a father is. At one end of the commitment spectrum is the *uncommitted father*. He takes little or no interest in parenthood. Children are a nuisance: a constant source of irritation and distraction from which he must try to escape as often as possible. He has never been able to cope with the demands they make upon him, and may consider that any involvement with them is 'unmanly'.

At the other end is the *overcommitted father*. He is so keen on parenthood that he tries to 'take over' from the mother, denying her any say in pregnancy, birth or childrearing. He is frankly envious of women's ability to bear children and unable to come to terms with the fact that there are differences between mothers and fathers — even the obvious biological ones.

The amount of commitment and kind of fatherhood a man adopts are not just the result of his personal decision. Attitudes are not

Traditional Overcommitted Father

formed in a vacuum, but are very susceptible to social pressures. A completely uninvolved approach towards fatherhood is not usually very acceptable. Although uncommitted fathers do exist, they tend to justify and explain their behaviour by reference to traditional values: 'I'd spend more time with my children if I could, but my job is so demanding that it just isn't possible.' It is not always easy to distinguish between the man who really subscribes to the values of traditional fatherhood and the uncommitted father who uses these values as an acceptable mask for his own attitudes.

It is also worth remembering that a man will change his degree of commitment to fatherhood during the course of his life. The attitudes of society at large may change as well. Some ages seem to have a greater commitment to the notion of father than others. Today there is certainly a greater readiness to talk about fatherhood than there has been for many years.

Most of the men I meet display a fair degree of explicit commitment towards fatherhood. This book is about them and their problems — about the *modern father* or *committed father*, who takes his fatherhood seriously, and wants to 'do it properly'. He is full of contradictions and uncertainties; his undoubted enthusiasm for family life can be coupled with moments of total indifference to them. He is indeed the uncertain father.

Women are keen on the committed father — or at least they think they are, although in practice he rarely measures up to their expectations. The committed father can sometimes discover a style of parenting which suits him, his family, and his personal circumstances; but more often he is forced into making a series of compromises which leave everyone feeling dissatisfied. What I want to find out is how we got into this uncomfortable position, why it is so unsatisfactory, and whether anything can be done to improve things.

2. The Making of the Modern Father

In the last chapter I came to some tentative conclusions about different ways of looking at fatherhood. I suggested that one of these, the traditional model — exemplified by the Victorian father — used to be dominant, but is now being challenged by other ways of looking at parenthood. In this chapter I want to look briefly at the rise of the Victorian father to discover in more detail what the traditional ideology actually is, and then go on to suggest some of the influences which have caused this view to be dethroned from its past pre-eminence.

Traditional fatherhood, with its emphasis on the authority of the father and a pronounced division of labour between father at work and mother at home, seems to have had its heyday in the aftermath of the industrial revolution. Until then the distinction between home and work was not so finely drawn as it is now. Much work was done at home or based in the home, and the family often worked together as an economic unit. The introduction of the factories changed things. Work had to done away from the home. The nature of work also changed, making it less appropriate for the family to work together as an economic unit. Because the workplace was unsuitable for babies and young children, childcare became a problem.

The industrial revolution also increased the earning power of many people — especially men. A man could now be able to earn enough to support a family on his own, and this became a mark of status. If a man was a 'success' then his wife didn't need to go to work as well. An ideology gradually developed which claimed that men should work and women should stay at home to solve the childcare problem.

Instead of being a worker a woman should now to aspire to motherhood. The invention of motherhood as a separate role, complete and sufficient unto itself, was underway. The converse of this was that 'fatherhood' as a separate role was also being emphasized. Stress was laid on the *differences* between men and women, and these became increasingly exaggerated by the spokesmen of the emerging middle classes.

> The man's power is the active, progressive, defensive. He is eminently the doer, the creator, the discoverer, the defender...But the woman's power is for rule, not for battle — and her intellect is not for invention or creation, but for sweet ordering, arrangement, and decision. (*John Ruskin*).

This new division of labour was enthusiastically taken up by the prosperous Victorian middle classes. It became the basis of a whole new way of looking at men and women. Feminist writers have pointed out how this demeaned and diminished women, but the effect on men has not been so frequently noticed.

While it would be a mistake to idealize the pre-industrial family, it does seem to have been a more integrated unit than in industrial times. By locking women inside the home the Victorians effectively locked men out. Just as women were deprived of experiences relating to production — such as power, creativity, adventure; so men were excluded from areas relating to reproduction — such as nurturing, caring, encouraging, supporting.

There were five qualities which, to a greater or lesser extent, characterized the ideal of the traditional father which the Victorians promoted:

Firstly, and most importantly, he should provide money for the home and family. It was the father's job to work; mother's to look after the family. The successful father provided well for his family, the unsuccessful did not. Indeed, if a woman had to work as well then her husband's emasculation was proclaimed to the world — he was clearly incompetent as a man as well as a father. A good father did not keep his money to himself but was generous to his children — indeed, this was one of the features of upper class Victorian fathers most remembered by their children.

This emphasis on material success required many men to spend long hours at work. Inevitably, they had little or no time for their families. It became increasingly difficult for a man to build a personal relationship with his children. Instead, his fatherhood had to be experienced at second hand, through his wife.

The father was also the mediator between the domestic and public domains. It was he who ventured out to become wise in the ways of the world. The home was insulated from the rude tumults outside, a haven of peace and delight; so the father became the only reliable channel of information about the wider world. He decided what the rest of the family should know and when they should remain ignorant.

The father was not only better informed than the mother, he also tended to be better educated and so could lay down standards of behaviour appropriate to the outside world. He took the responsibility for intellectual attainment and career success. The mother was responsible for more ethereal things:

> Woman, above all other educators, educates humanely. Man is the brain, but woman is the heart of humanity; he its judgment, she its feeling; he its strength, she its grace, ornament, and solace. (*Samuel Smiles*)

It was the father's job, too, to make sure that moral standards were kept. This was more true of the man who had been affected by the evangelical Christian revival than the man who embraced a traditional and conventional Anglicanism. The new piety led to an increased concern with the moral development of children. The father began to feel that it was his duty to make sure his children grew up with a proper sense of right and wrong. It was his job to be ultimately responsible for discipline.

Women were thought to be soft, gentle creatures who could not be expected to resort to harsh measures, should they become necessary. So, reluctantly but nobly, the father was forced to 'do the dirty work'. 'This will hurt me more than it will hurt you' has become a cliché, but perhaps there was an element of truth in it. The Victorian father, a model of propriety, was unable to see much of his children. When he did, he often had to stifle his natural affection in order to enforce compliance with this same propriety. It was not necessarily easy, nor did he necessarily enjoy it. But duty weighed very heavily with the Victorian father.

Finally. the Victorian father was concerned with preserving tradition and the existing social order. An important part of this was the upholding of appropriate gender behaviour. Boys should behave like young gentlemen, and girls like young ladies. The differences were quite clear and essential both to the orderly maintenance of society and to the personal well-being of the individual's concerns.

David Roberts has characterized the Victorian upper class father as being remote, sovereign, and benevolent. But if fatherhood was marked by its outward-looking, and authoritarian aspects, motherhood was just the opposite. It was the mother's job to run the home and take responsibility for the care and upbringing of the children.

> The home is the woman's domain — her kingdom, where she exercises entire control. Her power over the little subjects she rules there is absolute. They look up to her for everything. She is the example and model constantly before their eyes, whom they unconsciously observe and imitate. (*Samuel Smiles*).

The mother's responsibilty was not something to be taken lightly. If she was the cause of success then she could also be the root of all developmental evil. The idea that motherhood is a holy vocation managed to oppress women by its impossible demands and unwarranted assumptions about femininity; but it also oppressed men by excluding them from the home and consigning them to a life of work, conflict and politics.

Even though the Victorian ideal was very influential, it was probably only put into practice in relatively few homes. But these were the homes of the wealthy middle classes who usually tend to be the major opinion formers in Western society. Futhermore, it was supported by the establishment in the form of both Church and State. The traditional model is hierarchical: the father has authority over the mother, and the mother has authority over the children. Because of this it is very congenial to those who favour such a divison of authority in political or religious life.

The influence of the Victorian model continued long after the social system which gave it its prominence. But it was transformed in subtle ways in the generations which followed. The father's distance from the home was given even more emphasis, as was the mother's role within it. The consequence was that the father became to be viewed as almost irrelevant to his children.[3] His own parental role was ignored in favour of the part he could play in supporting his wife's parenting. So much so that in 1964 a prominent psychoanalyst could write that:

> ..father is needed at home to help mother to feel well in her body and happy in her mind...father is needed to give mother moral support, to be the backing for her authority, to be the human being who stands for the law and order which mother plants in the life of the child. (*Winnicott*, pp.114-115)

This writer, D.W. Winnicott, also sees the father as having a more sinister role to play:

> Besides, it is much easier for the children to be able to have two
> parents; one parent can be felt to remain loving while the other is
> being hated, and this in itself has a stabilizing influence... Every now
> and again the child is going to hate someone, and if father is not
> there to tell him where to get off, he will hate his mother and this
> will make him confused, because it is his mother that he loves most
> fundamentally. (p.114)

But even as this pronouncement was being made, the model of fatherhood
which it presented was being seriously challenged. Indeed, the criticisms
gained momentum to such an extent that in the course of just one
generation we have witnessed a remarkable transformation of attitudes.
The old attitudes have been undermined and, in some cases, swept away
altogether.

One of the most important factors underpinning this change has been
economic. You don't have to be an orthodox Marxist (which I'm not) to
recognize that a change in economic circumstances often has a profound
influence on social institutions. I have already suggested that it was
essentially just such a change — the Industrial Revolution — which led to
the pre-eminence of what we call 'the traditional father'. His primary duty
was to provide for his family; today a different set of economic conditions
mean that this is no longer such a priority for many fathers.

It is now easier to provide. The great wealth of the developed nations
means that few fathers have the sole task of keeping their children from
poverty. A father may be absent or incompetent, and his family will still
survive. Welfare payments will ensure that even if they are relatively poor
they will not starve or go without shelter.

We used to be in a situation where a man's success as a father was
measured primarily by his ability to keep his family from the breadline. Is
it now true that a good father provides more goods for his family than a
bad father? Some parents seem to think so, and do all they can to keep up
with the Joneses by providing their children with everything they ask for
— and most children have asked for the earth (at least) by the time they
have started school!

Even if you don't think it good for children to have all they want, the
pressures get stronger as the children get older. 'Charlie gets twice as much
pocket money as me, Dad.' You know that Charlie isn't typical; he has the
biggest allowance of anyone in the class, but this is little consolation. Not
that you approve of the amount of money that Charlie has to spend —
you certainly wouldn't let *your* child have as much. But if you were as

well-off as Charlie's dad then you could make that choice; as things are, you can't afford any more and the choice is removed from you. You don't believe that money can buy happiness, but even so you can't help feeling a little inadequate and guilty.

The fact that the father is no longer the sole provider may be a relief to some men, but it also undermines one of the pillars of traditional fatherhood. In addition it makes it harder to tell how 'good' a father a man is. If he provides adequately, he does no more than everyone expects of him. But the amount of his provision does not distinguish the adequate father from the inadequate father. If he gives his children lots of material goods, he is made to feel guilty by society because he is 'spoiling' them. If he witholds material goods he is made to feel guilty by his children for being 'mean'. Money has become part of the *Catch-22* of modern fatherhood.

But apart from the general increase in material goods, other economic factors have been at work. Changing patterns of employment have also had a dramatic effect on the old division between the female world of the home and the male world of work. More and more women are entering the market place and there is a constant upward trend of female employment. Increasingly, women don't need men to provide for them. If being able to provide for the family is a crucial part of the definition of fatherhood, then in this respect at least a woman can be as good a father as a man.

In fact, the picture is even bleaker for the traditional father. Not only is the rate of female employment increasing, but the rate of male *un*employment is also increasing. In more and more households the mother is showing not just that she can be as good a provider as the father, but that she can do it better. If a good father is one who provides, then an unemployed father is in danger of being a failed father.

The traditional model of fatherhood can be oppressive at times. Enforced unemployment is never pleasant, but the unemployed man who identifies himself as a traditional father cannot but come to feel himself a failure and a source of disappointment to both himself and his wife.

In many households where a man is unemployed, his partner is more able to get work than he — especially part-time work. If this happens, he will find himself at home looking after the children. He is likely, at least intially, to see this as compounding his defeat and humiliation. This is not helped by the attitudes displayed by officialdom — which often pretends that the traditional Victorian family patterns still exist after a century of social change. For instance, in Britain a family on a low income is entitled to a benefit payment called Family Income Supplement. However, in the case of a couple, "it must be the man who is in full-time work". Thus does the State compound the disadvantage felt by the father who is forced to stay at home.

In time such a man may come to discover delight and even fulfilment in his situation. Studies have shown that many unemployed men feel they have a closer relationship with their children because of the extra time they can spend with them, and some men I know would not go back to work if you paid them! But it is probably true to say that many men lose faith in themselves as fathers, at least initially.

A third employment-related factor has been a trend towards more flexible working patterns and a shorter working week. It is, I think, a mistake to assume that the only reason the traditional father saw little of his children was because he didn't want to, or thought it was unmanly. Often he simply didn't have the time. More free time has given many men the chance to get to know their children better; the chance to get home from work before the children have gone to bed.

The traditional division of labour has not only been affected by new economic circumstances. The ideology which used to underpin it has also been vigorously challenged from many quarters, of which one of the most influential has been the women's movement.

Those of us who grew up soon after the Second World War had very clear notions of what a father should do. We were brought up to believe that men and women had separate and clearly defined roles, and we accepted this without question. It all seemed to be perfectly simple.

We, as husbands and fathers (the two were inevitably supposed to go together), would go out into the hostile world, risk the rat race and accept its pressures so that we could earn bread for the family. Our wives (and mothers of our children) would stay at home, safe and protected from all the vicissitudes of the cruel world. They would care for all of us, happily doing those little tasks which turned a house into a home.

But even though our primary work was outside the home, there was a role we could play in bringing up our children. Indeed, a lot of us felt that our own fathers — many of them still emotionally scarred by the war — were too distant and uncaring. *We* would be around the house a bit more often and would make a real effort to be friends with our children. Yet even so, we basically saw fathering as a rather low-key affair. We learned most of what we knew from the movies; and there a father's main function seemed to be to vet his daughter's boyfriends when she brought them home (and to worry like mad when she didn't), and to play suitably

Traditional Uncommitted Father

manly rough-and-tumble games with our sons (so that they wouldn't get too attached to their mothers and grow up 'queer').

Most of us saw fatherhood only in terms of such peripheral activities. We didn't think of it as a proper job or a fulfilling state; for many it was a word with no real meaning. When a woman had a baby, she became a mother; when a man had a baby, he became the husband of a mother.

We never really questioned this Victorian division of labour — largely because it seemed essentially fair; though if we were pressed, we would have had to admit that women got the better of the bargain. It was clear that there were heavy penalties attached to being male — women lived longer, for one thing. And also it was easier for a woman: all she had to do was find some man to provide for her. This extra responsibility was a heavy burden, but — *noblesse oblige* — most of us were prepared to shoulder it manfully. And then a funny thing happened. Some women, just a few at first, started to say that it was *women* who had the raw end of the deal.

Men reacted in a variety of ways. There was, and still is, reactionary prejudice. There was, and still is, a desire to keep the privileges of power. There was, and still is, an inability to accept women as equals. But there was also surprise; the beginnings of understanding; and guilt. Many men had genuinely not realized that being at home with children was such a terrible thing as the feminists proclaimed it to be. But if it was so, then no man with a conscience could allow his wife to continue to suffer alone. So, out of a sense of duty, or simply to keep the peace and have a quiet life, some men started to do more around the house and to spend more time with the children.

They quickly realized that there were certain activities which had a great symbolic importance for women — changing nappies (diapers) was a prime example. So men started to change nappies. Being present at birth was another; so men started to be present at birth (though there was more to it than that, as we will see in chapters five and six). Guilt became the driving force which propelled men towards involvement in the home and family.

When they got there they discovered two things: firstly, that babies and children can be fun, and secondly that it is hard to be authoritarian when the baby has just puked all over you and you don't know where the clean baby clothes are! Because women were generally more skilled at childcare than men, it was almost impossible for the man to make decisions or take charge. The patterns of power and authority in the traditional family depend in part on the father being able to keep away from housework. Inevitably, when the man gets his hands dirty too, family life becomes more egalitarian.

Other changes have also contributed towards the establishment of new power relations within the home. Some research suggests that fathers are more authoritarian in large families than in small ones. He is more likely to be the final arbiter in disciplinary matters and will also tend to speak for the family when they are dealing with outsiders. In part this is simply because it is easier to treat a large family as a coherent group rather than as a collection of different individuals. (*Benson*, p.96).

This still seems to be the experience of those with larger families today. I have spoken to parents with five or more children and they frequently say that the more children you have, the more important discipline becomes. One mother put it this way:

> With one child, you can try to avoid confrontation, you can work round a problem, negotiate with them. There's no time to do that with five so you just end up being stricter.[4]

In fact, it is generally true that the larger any group becomes the more likely it is to develop centralized and formal authority structures. It is in just such situations that men seem more inclined than women to try to dominate the group. In chapter eleven we will see that some writers think that is part of men's biological make-up. So the trend towards smaller families may have played a part in the decline in openly authoritarian and patriarchal behaviour by many modern fathers.

Changing attitudes towards masculinity and femininity have also been very influential — again due largely to the influence of the women's movement. An increasing number of men have begun to question some of the more extreme masculine stereotypes that they grew up with. Tenderness and caring are not seen as necessarily 'effeminate'. These changes have made it easier for some men to become emotionally involved with their children — *and willing to express their involvement openly*.

There have been many strands in the cord which has led us through the maze from past certainty to present uncertainty. Women have achieved the potential for economic independence; men have more time to spend with their children; the old bargain between the sexes is now seen as based on exploitation rather than reciprocity; power relations within the family have altered; and men are able to develop and express the tender nurturing side of their natures.

But a word of caution is needed. Much has indeed changed, but much has also remained the same. It is worth taking another look, but this time with a rather more jaundiced eye.

For instance, although work patterns have changed, and more women are at work, the picture is still overwhelmingly traditional. Roughly equal numbers of men and women are in full-time employment before marriage, but a lot of women still give up work when they marry. Even more stop work in their first pregnancy and do not return until their youngest child reaches school age. Between a half and two-thirds of families with young children are still operating with the traditional division of labour.[5]

The women's movement may have affected some men, but there are many others who remain almost entirely untouched by it. They do not accept that society is patriarchal nor do they see any reason to feel guilt. On the contrary, they consider that women have always tried to have their cake and eat it. Now the women's movement wants a bigger cake! Such men see no reason to revise their opinions about sex roles or childcare. The traditional values suit them and they will continue to uphold them.

Other men go further, to become part of what Barbara Ehrenreich has called the "Flight from Commitment". She has suggested that running parallel to the women's movement, and even perhaps ahead of it, was an ad hoc and uncoordinated men's movement whose central battle cry was the rejection of 'the breadwinner ethic'. She argues that in the 1950s there was a firm expectation that a man should marry and support his wife. Anything else was immature and unmanly. But, starting in the mid-1950s, there was a revolt against conformism led by such diverse forces as Jack Kerouac and the Beat Generation, *Playboy* magazine, cardiologists who warned of the dangers of 'stress', and gurus of the sixties who preached the virtues of personal growth. All of these influences tended to work against the values of commitment and selflessness which made up the breadwinner ethic. The men who were touched by this movement were not likely to be enamoured of the responsibilities of fatherhood.

Many men have more free time nowadays, but this does not mean that they automatically spend more time with their families. Increased leisure has been accompanied by increased spending power. There is plenty of temptation to go to the pub after work, or to play squash or bridge, or to spend the evening in the club. Several studies have claimed to show that men still spend very little time with their children. One of the most famous — and most often cited — was that conducted by Freda Rebelsky and Cheryl Hanks. They attached a microphone to the baby's clothes and recorded the length of time when child and father were making noises to each other. This was done for 24 hours once a fortnight for the first three months of the child's life. The average came out as a mere 37.7 seconds a day! This figure is exceptionally low, and other American studies have shown a higher degree of involvement.[6]

Brian Jackson estimated that in 1975, "...half the fathers in Britain seldom see their young child, except over a busy breakfast, a complicated weekend or a welcome holiday." (p.23)

The reality of modern fatherhood is complex and often paradoxical. All generalizations are doomed to failure. In the rest of the book I shall look at little more closely at what it means to be a father today. Although I am concerned with all kinds of father I shall pay particular attention to the *committed father* — the man who wants to do his best as a father, but who may be uncertain about exactly what he is supposed to do. I will also concentrate most closely on the period from conception to the first few months after birth because it is this time which shows most clearly the nature of modern fatherhood and the pitfalls the modern father can encounter.

3. The Fascination of Fatherhood

Why do men become fathers? Is fatherhood simply an unfortunate byproduct of a careless and transitory pleasure, or do men actually want children? It's not a subject men talk about a great deal, and even when they do, there's not usually much articulate comment. Some men are open in their desire for children, but in our society most seem to be more ambivalent. They do want children — 'but not just yet'. Reasons for desiring parenthood differ according to circumstances, and even according to culture.

Children can have great economic value, especially in traditional societies. Among nomads, such as those of East Africa, as a man gets older and more successful his herds of cattle become larger and more difficult to look after. The assistance of sons is crucial to him because sons will work for nothing, just because they are kin, whereas other herdsmen will require some form of payment for their labour. Practical economics such as this often leads to boys being valued more than girls in societies like these. But girls have an economic and political role to play too, although it is less direct. Nomadic societies (and many others as well) are usually organized in family groups, where the family connection is traced in the male line. These groupings are called *lineages* and are the fundamental political groupings in such societies. Everyone belongs to the same lineage as his father. But it is a general rule that people from the same lineage must not marry. So if I have daughters they must leave my lineage and contribute their reproductive potential to another man's lineage; helping to build up his group so that it may become more powerful.

Marriages in such societies are usually arranged by the fathers of the bride and groom. Since marriage must always take place outside the lineage, it inevitably involves a relationship between two different families. There is no doubt that an astute man can arrange marriages for his children to provide him with alliances with other families which increase his own power and prestige. So a man may desire children in order to further his political ambitions. Of course, it is not only nomadic societies which make such 'dynastic' marriages. You have merely to look at the history of Europe, or the marriage patterns of wealthy families in the USA — or some of the more up-market soap operas — to see similar alliances and power plays being made.

Children may be of benefit to their parents in other ways as well — as a form of insurance for old age, for instance. If I have children then surely at least one of them will look after me when I am old? Many parents today deny this as a motive in their desire for a family — but will they not expect such support when they themselves are old? The ties of kinship are powerful. They involve obligations which are not based on short term considerations such as appear in commercial or legal transactions. Nor are they based on narrow self-interest. But there is usually an expectation that, in the end, things will balance out.[7] At the start of life parents pour time, money, energy and love into their children. At the end of life, most children feel obligated to repay some of this when their own parents need them.

Another part of the desire for children is less practical, but draws on deeper emotions. A man wants children, it is said, so that they can perpetuate his name: an attempt to cheat death. The individual dies, but his name is remembered by his children. They may, as in our society, actually carry his name — but even if they don't he knows that there will be someone to ensure that he is not forgotten.

In some societies it is believed that unless a man has someone to remember him, perhaps with sacrifices or other ritual displays, his spirit will not be able to rest easily. Such beliefs provide the basis of much that is commonly known as 'ancestor worship', although it doesn't usually involve worship in the sense that we use it.

We don't have ancestor worship in the West, but the feelings which underpin it speak to us too. Children offer us the prospect of continuity; they are the thread which connects us to the future. Because of this they help to keep us from feeling too isolated and alone. We know that, through them at least, we fit into a wider pattern of society which reaches out through space and time.

This sense of reaching into the future can have a profound effect on a man. The birth of my firstborn, Mark, made a great impact on my

Modern (Active) but Overcommitted Father

attitudes towards the future and towards death. Suddenly the future became more real and important. I began to worry more about the possibilities of a nuclear war. No longer was it enough to hope selfishly for peace to last until my own natural death; I now had another generation to care about. This was one of the most important factors which led ultimately to a radical shift in my political and social views. I have not explored this in any detail with other men, but it would be interesting to know whether the birth of a baby commonly has similar effects on the new father's world-view.

The suggestion that children provide a type of immortality has recently been revived by evolutionary biologists. Since Darwin it has been generally accepted that the way to judge the 'success' of a species is to consider whether or not it continues to exist — in other words, how effectively it reproduces itself. More recently, this approach has been applied by Richard Dawkins to individuals — or more especially to individuals' genes, those chemical structures which contain the code which determines how the cells in your body are put together.

The argument, briefly, is this. If there was a gene which tended to make its carrier reluctant to have children it would not reproduce itself, and would soon die out. It is therefore most unlikely that such a gene could exist. On the other hand a gene which made any creature carrying it very keen to reproduce would obviously stand a very good chance of being around for many generations to come.

Specific genes to encourage or discourage people from having children almost certainly do not exist. But the argument still applies. If my genes manage to reproduce themselves they are successful; otherwise they will vanish from the earth and other, 'fitter', genes will take over. So the very fact that our ancestral genes have already survived long enough to have been reproduced in us means that they must be quite good at reproducing themselves. The chances are therefore that we are all 'genetically programmed' to want to reproduce ourselves — or rather to reproduce our genes. Thus men 'want' to have children because they cannot help it. Reproduction has become a biological imperative.

It is not the physical structure of the genes which survives from generation to generation, but faithful copies of them. If survival is all that matters, then the more copies there are the better chance the genes have of surviving. So, at first sight we might assume that the more children you have the better your genes' survival chances. But things are not quite so simple. It does my genes no good to survive in my children unless the children also live long enough to reproduce. So I must try to make sure that at least some of my children do not die before they become mature. There are two possible strategies which I might adopt to help bring this about.

Firstly, I could simply take every reproductive opportunity I find so that I had as many offspring as possible. I wouldn't bother to waste time looking after them, but would simply hope that at least some would surive to adulthood and be able to reproduce themselves. Alternatively I could have just a few children and concentrate all my resources on trying to ensure that they grow up safely.

In general, biological theory might suggest that men should be more promiscuous than women. Since females have a limited number of ovulations, and do not usually produce children more frequently than one every nine months (although a woman could have two sets of premature quintuplets in a year!) they have less to gain by having many different mates. It is probably better for a woman to concentrate her resources on looking after the children she does have. Men, on the other hand, produce millions of sperm per ejaculation and could father several new babies every day. Why should they ever bother to do anything else?

There are, however, several biological reasons why men do not simply adopt a promiscuous reproductive strategy. In most cases, a child will have a better chance of survival if it has two people to look after it than if there is only one. So a mother, who as we have seen is likely to invest in her children's survival, has a vested interest in trying to keep a man around to help care for her children. She may offer sufficient inducements to him to persuade him to stay with her and help bring up the children.

It is often in the man's own reproductive interest to invest in his children too. Consider a population where none of the men did anything to help look after their children. Any man who decided to go against the normal state of affairs and invest in his offspring would immediately gain an advantage over the others. More of his children would survive to adulthood than those of the other men, and so more of his genes would go into the next generation's gene pool. If his children adopted the same strategy they too would have his success, and this set of genes would gradually dominate the whole population.

There is a limit to this, though. Suppose we had a population where all men helped to look after their own children. Any man who decided to go against this norm and cuckold other men would now gain. He would be able to invest all his energies in trying to persuade women to have his babies, while being secure in the knowledge that all these babies would be looked after by the partners of those women. In this case his genes would do better than everyone else's and they would gradually come to dominate the population.

Clearly, in simple biological terms, if everything else is equal neither of these two extremes provides a stable strategy. Richard Dawkins has calculated that in certain circumstances a ratio of eight promiscuous types to five faithful ones will allow each kind to do equally well. In real life things are more complicated. None of us consciously adopts either strategy, and we all know men who try bit of each — although not usually in any conscious attempt to increase their reproductive success!

Biological arguments like this can give us valuable insights, but they are inadequate to explain all the complexities of human behaviour. Many men do not want children and remain childless all their lives. Are their genes defective in terms of reproductive drive? And if so, how did they ever get to be born themselves? In human beings culture and biology interact in such complicated ways that simple theories are almost always wrong. The importance of biology is that it can tell us about some of the innate tendencies which may underpin our behaviour and which may restrict the range of choice we have, and show the limits within which we can try to modify our behaviour.

Biological and economic reasons may help to explain why men want to be fathers, but they by no means exhaust the possibilities. The man who feels that his own life has been spoiled by lack of education or social advantages may wish for children so that they might pursue the career he was never able to have. 'My kids will have all the opportunities I never had,' he says, and he devotes the rest of his life to their welfare, trying to re-live his own life vicariously through his children. Most men do not go so far, but it can be hard to resist this particular temptation.

Having a child may be important to a man's self-image in other ways — for instance, it demonstrates his sexual competence in a way that nothing else can. No matter how good a man might be in bed, no matter how many women he has slept with, unless he has actually sired a child his potency remains only potential and not demonstrated. Men are notoriously insecure in their sexuality, but a man with a child is able to relax a bit. Few men express this feeling openly, but I think it lies deep for many of us.

> At confirmation of pregnancy I wanted to tell the world that I'd 'rung the bell', whereas Sandy wanted to wait until any early complications were passed. (*John*)

This takes us back to that basic meaning of the verb 'to father': to sire, to be the producer of the spermatazoon which fertilizes the egg which becomes the child. I said at the beginning of the book that this implies a single act requiring little effort, and absolutely no committment over a period of time. Yet it does not mean that the act of fathering is without any other significance. For John, as for most men, it was not the *primary* reason for wanting a child. But for some men in some cultures it is enough — just as there are women who want a child simply in order to demonstrate their femininity.

Other men want children, not principally for themselves, but for their wives. We live in a society where many women expect to find their main fulfilment in the bearing and nurturing of children. Men are aware of this, and many feel it their duty to have children for this reason. They would not take the step of their own accord, perhaps; but under pressure from their partner, or out of consideration for her desires, they acquiesce.

It is still hard for a woman to be accepted as a success if she has not had children. Even if childlessness is a voluntary decision, she is accounted unfortunate or even selfish — not a proper woman. The same does not apply to a man. A man can go through life childless without anyone else openly noticing his lack. He may feel it deeply himself, but there is little social stigma. Thus it is usually the woman who takes the initiative in decisions about children. Furthermore, the major share of childcare responsibilities is still taken by women and seen as 'women's work', and many men feel that it is only right that women should have the major say in decisions about children.

Another relevant point is that the nature and control of contraception has changed. Traditionally, when the sheath was the principal form of contraceptive, men were responsible for birth prevention. But they did not always find it convenient or conducive to pleasure (one man described it as being like washing your hands while wearing rubber gloves) and were often lax in their precautions. Since a man can 'kiss and run', women gradually took over responsibility for contraception.

At first this seemed like a great development to most men. Contraception had always been seen as a chore. The newer methods of cap, pill and coil seemed to offer liberation for men as well. Women were now more accessible, and there was nothing — however well lubricated and 'super-sensitive' — to interfere with pleasure. It even saved money! But there was a catch.

What was not always recognized — by men anyway — was that whoever is in control of contraception is also in control of conception.

Some men leave decisions about babies to their partners simply because they have little choice. How easy it is for a woman 'accidentally' to forget to take the pill one day. And how easy too, to assume that everything will probably be alright — especially if you don't mind if it isn't. Sometimes the deception is blatant, but much more often there is a conspiracy of silence; one of those little games we play to save face and make life more interesting.

I had always wanted to have two children, long before I married Shirley. She also wanted children, but never really said how many she wanted (or perhaps I never listened when she expressed different ideas from my own). Our first two children were both boys, which was a bit of a disappointment to me as I was very keen to have a daughter. Nevertheless I still did not want to go beyond my 'ideal' number of two. But Shirley had by now decided that she wanted more children; two were not enough. Despite the possibility of getting my much-wanted daughter, I still refused to agree.

One day (or was it more than one?) Shirley forgot to take her contraceptive pill. She now says that she mentioned this to me and that I agreed that there was little risk of her getting pregnant. I have no recollection of this at all, and the inevitable pregnancy came as a surprise to me. This was nine years ago and it is now no longer possible to discover whose version is correct. But perhaps we were both right: perhaps there was a silent conspiracy between us, and this was the best way for each to save face. Real life decisions are often made this way.

Anyway, the story had a happy ending, for the new baby was the little girl I wanted and I have no regrets at all about being proved wrong. Shirley now claims that she was always sure it would be a girl, and that she had always wanted two boys and a girl (so that the girl would be able to go out with the friends of her older brothers)!

Another reason why men want children came up the other night when I was talking with Mark, my elder son. "Don't have children when you grow up," I joked, "they're too much trouble." He laughed. "I'm going to treat my children *properly* when I grow up, Dad." How many children have said or thought that? I know I did. Perhaps this is one of the earliest influences on our decisions to have children — a desire to avoid the mistakes (real or imagined) that our own parents made.

I wanted to have children because it seemed an important and creative thing to do. Many men feel this way, even though it is not fashionable to admit it in some circles. But, from my experience of talking with parents, I would say that one important difference between men and women is that *women tend to want babies, while men are more likely to want children.* Of course there are exceptions, but in general when men think of fatherhood they tend to think of spending time with older children.

Fatherhood means playing cricket on the beach, taking Johnny to his first football game, helping Julia with her maths homework. Before they have children, many men think of fatherhood as if it were being like a favourite uncle: full of indulgence and good humour, but with little real commitment. It is an attractive image — the benevolent side of the traditional father stereotype — which no doubt contributes to some men's desire to have children.

The 'uncle' image is an appealing one for many men, especially in its lack of commitment. The uncle can hand the child back and clear off when the going gets tough. A father cannot (should not?) do that.

Commitment frightens many young men; more so perhaps than young women.

> Susan wanted to have a baby at least a year before I did. Being a father was a rather frightening thought to me. I kept waiting to be more together, to have my life somehow be more resolved. (*David Steinberg*, p.19)

A book written for fathers in the 1950s lists seven 'standards' to which a young man must measure up before he can do an adequate job of fathering. These include having a sense of reality, the capacity to stand disappointment without sulking, being consistently engaged in doing something worthwhile, being cooperative, able to think of someone other than himself, and being willing to surrender present advantage for the sake of long-range goals. At the end of this impressive list the authors conclude that, "Prospective fatherhood tests your emotional maturity"! (*English & Foster*, p.12) It is little wonder that some men hesitate before having children.

Yet paradoxically, this can also be a major factor in a man's decision to have children. He may see it, consciously or unconsciously, as a necessary step in growing up. Having children ties you down, makes you accept your responsibilities. The responsibility factor is connected with the manhood one too. Having children means that you're a real man, not a boy any more. This can extend to attitudes towards the relationship between partners. Children, it is said, cement a marriage in a way that nothing else can. Certainly, in many societies a marriage is not completed or finally accepted until the birth of the first child. We do not formalize this in the

Western world, but divorce before any children are born is considered a less serious break than afterwards. Having children adds to the responsibilities of the couple. They ought now to try more seriously to 'settle down for the sake of the children.'[8]

An interesting perspective on why men want children can be found in David Owens' study of men's reactions to the fact that they were unable to have children. Owens interviewed some British working class men shortly after their first visit to an infertility clinic. When he asked them why they wanted children, most found it difficult at first to give any clear answer. It was just 'natural' to have children. Further questioning began to provide rather more detail.

Children were seen as a potential source of enjoyment and companionship when older and as 'fun' when babies. Boys were particularly sought after as companions in sport or recreational activities, but daughters, too, were felt important for a complete family. There was more stress on this, emotional, side of fatherhood than on more traditional values such as wanting an heir, or someone to care for the father in old age, or to provide any form of 'immortality'. Coupled with this was lack of real concern about the effects of having children. The men acknowledged that children would be expensive and would cause a change of lifestyle, but this was just accepted as an inevitable consequence of parenthood. There was no idea of 'investment for the future' or any real investigation of the true impact of such changes.

Children were also seen by these men as being essential to a proper marriage, and especially important in providing an opportunity for their wives to become mothers. Becoming a mother would inevitably be fulfilling, and was perceived as being crucial to a woman's development. When the men were questioned about their feelings towards their own possible infertility they were much less concerned with their performance as men than as husbands. There was some concern with masculinity — one man denied any worries about his own virility or manhood, but his wife said that he had taken to heart his brothers' remarks that, "you haven't proved yourself yet like we have". Yet overwhelmingly the men were worried that they might have let their wives down, depriving them of the chance of motherhood. One man summed it up:

> If the [sperm] test was negative, most probably I would have said I
> would have divorced her, because if you deprive a woman of a child,
> then you are depriving her of something which is very, very
> important to her, and no matter what my wife would have said to
> have eased my feelings on the subject whether she actually meant

that, it didn't matter or not. I would have felt uneasy especially when we were with other people's children, and I might have divorced her, but for her own sake. (p.83)

The desire to father is complex. Biology, economics, social expectations, and desire for personal growth can all contribute. But even those men who openly admit to wanting children have very little idea of the implications of their decisions. With the new ideology of involved fatherhood presenting itself as an option, many men find this period, when the thought of fatherhood becomes a fact, very stressful and challenging.

4. The Pregnant Father

Pregnancy can be a very worrying and emotionally intense experience for a man – which is odd when you consider that men don't get pregnant. Nevertheless it's true, as Greg's story shows.

I met Greg because his wife, Helen, phoned me one evening. She was worried about his reaction to her pregnancy. Greg is a kitchen equipment salesman in his mid-thirties who had been very successful in his job, always exceeding his sales quotas and often winning bonuses and trips abroad. According to Helen, he had been a confirmed batchelor and was somewhat taken by surprise by their recent marriage, let alone that he was on the verge of becoming a father. It seemed to be having a drastic effect on his life.

Helen was concerned that Greg seemed unable to cope with the approaching baby. According to her, he had changed dramatically during the pregnancy. She felt that he was not able to acknowledge these changes properly, and wouldn't talk about them. He also didn't want to touch her 'bump'. Greg's work had suffered as well. His sales performance had declined and he had just received a letter from his firm saying that if he wasn't able to achieve his sales quota they would fire him.

As I talked with Helen, it transpired that Greg was showing several other unusual symptoms. He came home from work tired and listless, and he complained of frequent headaches. He had become much more clinging, wanting to be cuddled constantly. And despite his increased interest in her, he also seemed to be paying more attention to other women.

Helen was convinced that Greg's main trouble was his inability to talk to anyone about his problems. She kept asking him what the matter was, but he consistently denied any problem. There was obviously a fundamental difference in attitude between them which would not be easy to bridge. This seems to be a common distinction between men and women today. Women feel that 'talking things over' must necessarily be a good thing, and that failure to do so is itself the sign of a problem. Although some men agree, the majority see no need to discuss emotional experiences. Strong silent suffering is still man's way.

Partly at Helen's urging, I met Greg a few weeks later in a pub near his home. He didn't strike me as being weighed down by the burdens of pregnancy. Indeed, he seemed pleased with the opportunity to talk about it, and was very positive about the forthcoming birth and his hopes for his new baby. Nevertheless, despite his openness, Greg's reaction to Helen's pregnancy was definitely being expressed in both physical and emotional changes. Greg may have been a little unusual in the *number* of symptoms he displayed, but many men will have similar experiences during pregnancy.

Many people express surprise that men suffer from pregnancy symptoms, but surely the surprising thing is that they suffer so few. Not only is pregnancy a time of stress and anxiety — with worries about whether the baby will be alright, whether it will be possible to cope financially, and so on — but it is also a time when many men experience major changes in attitude. Looked at in the terms of commitment and style of fathering as discussed in chapter one, most men become more committed and adopt a less traditional attitude towards fatherhood during the course of the pregnancy. The diagram shows the sort of movement (from **x** to **o**). They start with little commitment to fatherhood and with traditional attitudes, and move to become much more committed and keen on a more active style of fathering.

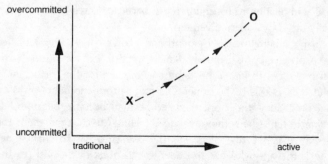

Not everyone follows this path, of course. I was more committed to fatherhood than many of my contemporaries, although my views were just as traditional as theirs. Some men may even become less committed and more traditional as the pregnancy develops. Nevertheless, both my experiences of talking with men and research findings suggest that a large number of men follow this sort of development. Women also undergo changes of attitude during pregnancy, similar in many cases to those experienced by men. But there is a major difference.

Having a baby is a very direct experience for a woman. Pregnancy lasts nine months and has an obvious physiological purpose, giving the fetus enough time to develop to a viable state. But pregnancy also provides a time of transition and preparation for motherhood. If a woman became a mother overnight, within 24 hours of conception, she would find it very hard to cope with the change in her status. Even with a nine month waiting period the reality of parenthood can be quite a shock!

Pregnancy is also a time a transition for a man, but for him there are no obvious physical changes to mirror the emotional transition to parenthood. There is no way of telling that a man is going to have a baby, even if it is due the very next day. People don't stop in the street and say, 'Oh look! A pregnant man. It won't be long now by the look of him!' For a man, the transition to parenthood is essentially an emotional experience — something which many men find particularly difficult to come to terms with since we are notoriously ill at ease with feelings; being much more at home with physical and practical things. This is one of the most important lessons of pregnancy because one of the differences between fatherhood and motherhood is just that: while motherhood is direct, based on the mother's emotional *and* physical involvement with the child, the father's relationship tends to be more diffuse, at one remove. The father often has more difficulty in relating to his children just because his relationship is not based initially on a physical involvement.

As a man's commitment to parenthood grows it is not enough for him to leave pregnancy as a purely female experience. He wants to be involved in it, to 'get to know' his baby and prepare for the forthcoming changes. But how is this to be done? The more pronounced the physical signs of her pregnancy, the more alienated he may become, because it is not happening to him. She is the one who is feeling the changes; she is the one everybody makes a fuss of; she is the one who has to change her lifestyle; she is the one who has to undergo the ritual of the visit to the clinic. These experiences may not be pleasant, but they all help to mark out the pregnant woman as someone special; someone undergoing a major life change. And because these are the ways we mark the transition to parenthood, men also need to experience them.

Many societies adopt a ritual strategy which helps the prospective parents get used to the idea of having a child, and become involved with the unborn. For instance, on the Andaman Islands in the Indian Ocean, the unborn child is given a name early in the pregnancy. From that time onward, until some weeks after the baby is born, no-one is allowed to call the expectant mother and father by their own names. Instead they must be called by means of the child's name: 'mother of so-and-so' or 'father of so-and-so'. They are also both obliged to abstain from eating certain foods. In this way the father's identification with the pregnancy is continually and publicly acknowledged. (*Radcliffe-Brown*, p.146)

In the West we generally ignore such obvious and public ritual solutions to our problems. So men adopt various other, unconscious, strategies to help their identification with the baby. Some undergo physical changes, which mimick women's pregnancy symptoms. Others alter their lifestyle, or use the pregnancy as an opportunity to reflect on their priorities in life. Pregnancy is a time of great change and uncertainty for many men, perhaps made worse by the fact that society as a whole does not acknowledge the powerful effect it can have on them.

It seems to me that men in the West are adopting private rituals in order to compensate for the lack of public ritual. The name given to such changes in lifestyle or behaviour, whether public or private, is couvade. This term is used by psychologists and anthropologists to refer to a wide range of such changes which can happen during pregnancy and through to the period shortly after birth.[9]

The most dramatic couvade symptoms are physical. Sometimes they can be quite bizarre and extreme. One 38-year-old man had a variety of symptoms during each of his wife's six pregnancies. During the first he had morning sickness and also severe and persistent tooth-ache, which led to him having all but eight of his molars extracted. On the day his child was born he was seized by a severe stomach ache. This gripped him for an hour or so while he sat on the lavatory. He subsequently found out that the pain left him at just about the time his baby was born! The symptoms were similar during each pregnancy, with morning sickness, loss of appetite, abdominal pains and toothache being the most common. He was also displayed great anxiety about his wife's pregnancies — which were all free from complications — and felt very guilty about causing her to be in such a dangerous state (*Enoch & Trethowan*). Midwifery lore has long associated pregnancy with teeth, and approaching fatherhood with tooth-ache; is this

Modern (Active) but Uncommitted Father

perhaps because the extraction of a tooth is a natural symbol for the birth (extraction) of a baby?

Other men have less severe or painful symptoms, but they are just as real. Some suffer from morning sickness, others put on weight or get severe abdominal pains. Brian Jackson found that the men he spoke to also encountered wind, constipation, backache, "a feeling of fullness in my stomach", strong changes of taste in food and drink, and new, broken, sleep patterns. Jackson estimated that 34 men, out of the 100 he interviewed, had some physical symptoms — although only seven actually identified these as being related to the pregnancy. Other studies have estimated that as many as 60% of men experience some physical signs of pregnancy.

Why do men display such reactions? Stress is commonly cited as one reason. Betty Parsons is an antenatal teacher. She tells the following story:

> One man came to one of my Fathers' Evenings very reluctantly. His wife had warned me that he was extremely nervous. "He just doesn't want to know." she said. For several weeks he had been suffering from a very irritating rash that had not responded to treatment; his doctor called it his 'pregnancy rash'. As he left the Fathers' Evening he said to me: "I feel as if a burden's been lifted now that I understand the whole procedure. What a miracle it all is." Two days later his rash had disappeared! (p.28)

Physical symptoms are only the tip of the couvade iceberg. Many men rethink their attitudes to work during pregnancy. Work often provides the core of a man's existence; he has been brought up to value it above all things. Pregnancy forces a new evaluation of priorities. The prospect of a new life and a new creative responsibility is very powerful. After all, a job is just a job; a new life is altogether more important — especially if it is a part of you.

> I must admit I lost a certain amount of my involvement in my work, once we'd conceived the child. I started sort of seeing my family as a lot more important. My job now takes second precedence over my family whereas before my job was the important thing and my marriage was secondary. (*Andy*)[10]

This rearrangement of priorities has consequences for fatherhood in the months and years to come. It is important not to underestimate its power or seriousness. Greg, the kitchen salesman, nearly lost his job. He didn't feel that any major change had taken place, simply that his job wasn't quite so all-important any more. But this small change was enough to send him from super-salesman to below par in a few months.

Paradoxically, there is another common — but quite different — reaction to pregnancy felt by many men. A man may be overwhelmed by the forthcoming financial responsibility. He feels quite unable to cope, especially if his partner will be giving up work after the birth. This too can change a man's attitudes to work. He may feel the need to work longer hours in order to earn more, and the extra responsibility means that it is now more important to hang onto his job. He must become more conscientious, less able to rock the boat.

> I've always been one if the gaffer is funny with me, I've always told him what to do and walk out. There have been a few firms I've just finished from normally. I don't like to be dictated to. Since the wife has been pregnant, I've had to knuckle down a bit. I still speak my mind, but don't say 'get stuffed'. (Quoted in *Richman*, p.99)

A study undertaken for the British Equal Opportunities Commission asked nearly three hundred fathers about work and the impact of children. Only a few had actually changed the number of hours they worked as a result of having a child. Most of these men spent less time at work. The researchers also asked the men whether they wanted to change their hours. One in four would have liked to have worked fewer hours, and one in nine would have liked to work longer. Those who wanted to work less were equally divided between manual and non-manual workers but those who wanted to work longer were three times as likely to be manual workers — a good illustration of the greater amount of financial pressure a baby can put on working class families (*Bell* et al).

Not all reactions to pregnancy are so weighty. Many men engage in 'nesting' activity. They suddenly take an interest in the home; noticing that the place needs decorating. The most obvious sign of all is the preparation of the nursery. Even a very macho man can suddenly fall in love with pastel shades and pretty patterns. Perhaps it gives him an opportunity to explore the 'feminine' side of his nature without any risk to his self-image. After all, it's 'for the baby' or 'for the wife', not for him; so it's OK.

Some buy a pet, or start treating the pets they already have as if they were babies; picking them up and cuddling them — even using baby talk to them. Others show a new interest in babies, especially if there are relatives with young children. He suggests more visits to them, and perhaps manages to be there when the baby is being passed around for a cuddle. Inevitably someone will tease him and suggest that he has a turn at holding the baby. Many men have absolutely no experience of how to deal with young children and there are few funnier or more touching sights than to see an inexperienced man pick up a baby. He holds it slightly away from his body, arms tensed, watching intently as if it might either explode or else fall to pieces in his arms. It is a mixture of tenderness, concern and downright panic.

A man's attitudes and behaviour during pregnancy will obviously depend a lot on his attitude to the forthcoming birth. Perhaps the pregnancy was unintended. For some this will be a happy accident, for others a disaster. Some accept it stoically as a fate to be endured, others acknowledge it joyously as God's will. Things are different if the pregnancy was planned. Then, sexual intercourse assumed a new purpose; a purpose beyond simple pleasure. The union of seed and egg was intended, wished for, longed for perhaps; and because of this, making love will never be quite the same again.

But whether the baby was wished for or not, most men find that pregnancy changes their attitudes towards sex. Some men find the fact that they have demonstrated their own fertility quite exciting.

> It was sort of like the rutting season. I didn't do anything, but I was aware of myself being much more randy towards other women during that time. (*John*)

This may also be because of a sense of lost opportunities; a feeling that now you've burned your boats and are irrevocably committed to your partner. It's not that most men want to be unfaithful or break off the relationship at this time, but rather that they can feel very hemmed in by the pressures and responsibilities of approaching parenthood. A few may actually translate the thought into the deed, but for most it remains a vague feeling of generalized desire.

For some couples sex becomes better; they make love more often and more intensely. Many women find that, provided that they suffer no serious physical pregnancy symptoms, their own libido increases as pregnancy progresses. Masters and Johnson found that the majority of women in their study experienced an increase of the sex drive at around four to five months of pregnancy. Inevitably, many men find their partner's increased enthusiasm infectious. There is also a new lack of inhibition for many couples — after all, there is now no need to worry about contraception; no chance of an unexpected or unwanted pregnancy. Many men find the sheath an unsatisfactory contraceptive because it interferes with sensation, but also feel either anxious about the safety of methods such as the cap or guilty about the side effects of the pill or coil. The chance to lay aside all these worries during pregnancy is most appealing.

Lack of worry is one factor; the desire for greater closeness is another. When asked what effect the new baby would have, the most common answer given by a group of men surveyed at one hospital was that it would create a family. But the second most common response was that the new baby would restrict life; that it would mark the end of a carefree existence. Many men feel both of these responses quite strongly. A man may be drawn closer to his partner during pregnancy, not only because he senses the development of a new stage in their relationship — becoming a family rather than just a couple — but also because he senses the end of an old intimacy. He may want to have a last fling with her, a kind of second honeymoon before it is all too late.

But such feelings are not necessarily translated into sexual activity. Masters and Johnson found that 31 out of the 79 expectant fathers they interviewed gradually ceased sexual activity as the pregnancy progressed. Many men are afraid of hurting the baby, or causing a miscarriage, or in some way bringing 'bad luck' on the pregnancy.

Most of the baby books are not very supportive: they simply insist that such fears are groundless. There is, they say, no reason at all to stop intercourse unless you notice vaginal bleeding. They treat a lessening of sexual activity as a 'problem' which must be cured, instead of accepting the possibility that it is a normal and common male reaction to pregnancy. Because of this a man who 'suffers' from this 'problem' may feel either stupid or a failure — especially if his partner becomes more physical during pregnancy.

Some men worry that they will hurt the baby in a very direct and physical way. As the fetus gets larger and more active, you can become very aware during intercourse of just how short a distance there is between the tip of the penis and the baby only a few inches away in the uterus. The books, of course, tell us that there is no rational reason to worry. The cervix (neck of the uterus) is closed with a plug of mucus and the baby is wrapped in the membranes, and so is quite isolated from the outside world. Nevertheless, the worries continue. I even heard of a man who worried that the baby would put its hand through the cervix and grab his penis during intercourse! This too may be foolishness, but it certainly isn't an inducement to passion.

The reasons for male lessening of interest in sex are manifold. I think that in part it is another couvade symptom. By abstaining from normal sexual activity the man 'marks' the time of pregnancy as being special, and so involves himself in it more. It is worth remembering that men often see sex as debilitating or dangerous. Magicians and initiates are often instructed to abstain before undertaking a demanding exercise. Soldiers pass on the rumour that bromide is being put in the tea to diminish their sexuality before a battle. Athletes are kept isolated from wives and girlfriends the night before a big competition or during a tour. Whatever the physical reasons, abstaining from sex is one way men have of preparing for some great endeavour. And what greater event could there be than the forthcoming birth of your own child?

A man also has to come to terms with his partner's new role. She is becoming a mother. Not *his* mother of course, but because of his own deep involvement the distinctions may get a bit blurred. It is well known that you shouldn't have sex with a mother, so perhaps its best to lay off for a while until things have sorted themselves out. This isn't a problem near the surface for most men, though some are aware of it; but it is true that quite a lot of men start to behave in a rather babyish way, wanting to be 'mothered' by their partners. Perhaps this is because they find it hard to face up to the responsibility of fatherhood, perhaps because they are 'rehearsing' for the more tender and nurturing role they will adopt when the baby comes. Whatever the reason, if a man starts to treat his wife more like a mother figure he may well find it harder to make love to her because of this.

There may be other, even more fundamental, reasons for men to feel wary of sex during pregnancy. There may be some fear, not of the baby, but of the mother. Woman's fertility has been held in awe by men since the dawn of time. Men have tried to control it, mimic it, and deny it. But still it remains — the one power that we can never have. It is not surprising that some men are a little reticent in the presence of pregnancy. For it is during pregnancy that the power of fertility is most obviously displayed; that the physical differences between men and women are most openly shown. She changes, swells, matures; he stays the same, pedestrian, unable to catch her up. The wonder is not that so many men feel diffident about intercourse during pregnancy, but rather that so many are able to use the experience to develop a new closeness.

Lack of intercourse does not necessarily mean the end of physical relationship. Even though men often fail to distinguish between sexuality and sensuality, many are able to use pregnancy as a time to explore new ways of loving.

> My wife went totally off any sort of sex during the pregnancy,
> almost as if the act of procreation sort of made any further attempts
> unnecessary. But I felt no sort of deep frustration or anything. It was
> sufficient just that we were together. And we had sensual
> relationships, beautiful times, just sort of massaging her tummy and
> feeling the baby moving and just going to sleep with my arms sort
> of round holding the baby as well. (*Andy*)

These new expressions of sensuality can be a reflection of the move
towards a new equality in the relationship and a preparation for the power
sharing which is characteristic of the active father.

> It was an incredibly sexy period. I mean, we both felt really great
> about ourselves and about our lives; and part of my involvement
> with the baby took a fairly sort of sexual turn. I would massage Kate
> and Kate's tummy with baby oil and it was really nice. (*Stuart*)

This new interest in *her* body is mirrored, for some men, by a new interest
in their own. Studies of US airmen showed that they tended to become
more health conscious during pregnancy; exercising more, cutting down
on smoking, and in some cases drinking more milk! But not everyone finds
pregnancy a sufficient excuse for taking better care of themselves:

> My mother-in-law, luckily she's in Australia, thinks I should stop
> smoking for the sake of the baby. And my answer is if I can't stop
> smoking for the sake of myself, how the hell does she expect me to
> stop smoking for the sake of the baby? (*Ian*)

When we were expecting our first child I borrowed an obstetrics textbook
from the local library. It was full of pictures and stories of what might go
wrong, so I didn't show it to Shirley because I felt it might upset her. The
book wasn't actually much help to me, but I read it because I had a great
need to know about pregnancy and birth. Many men have a similar need
but in my experience they rarely express it until after the birth. There are
now several books on the market written expressly for the expectant father.
One or two of them are quite useful, although few really address
themselves to the father's needs. Most of them are probably bought by
women and given to men.

One of the best ways of preparing for parenthood is to attend
antenatal classes. Most hospitals or clinics provide them, as do private
organizations such as the International Childbirth Education Association in

the US and other parts of the world, the National Childbirth Trust in the UK, or Parents Centres in Australia and New Zealand. Nearly all antenatal courses welcome men to at least one class and many, especially the private ones, include them in the whole course. Yet men rarely go willingly, if at all.

Some men feel that the whole thing is women's business and simply don't want to interfere. Others *know* it's women's business because their partners don't want them to interfere. And there are those who know that they are welcome, but feel that it's a bit unmanly to sit down with a lot of women and talk about babies. Despite the apparent unwillingness, many men are really quite keen, but worry about possible loss of face. It is here that the excuse, 'I only came because she wanted me to' can be so convenient. It provides a way of having your cake and eating it, and this can be important to the man who is still having difficulty in coming to terms with a new involvement in family matters.

Many men are reluctant to attend antenatal classes simply because they feel that the classes will not be relevant to them. And they are often correct. Many hospitals and clinics hold their classes during the day, when it is hard for most men to get time off to attend. But at present, the man who does manage to get there is unlikely to be heartened by his reception. Either he will be resented or he will be matronized (antenatal classes are almost exclusively run by women).

> I only went to one class. We were supposed to be going up to look at where we would actually have our babies. And then, all of a sudden the lady that was organizing it all said tup to look at where we would actually have our babies. And then, all of a sudden the lady that was organizing it all said to me, "Oh I'm terribly sorry, you can't come up." Which amazed me. There were twelve women and myself and she said, "There won't be room up there you see." I was rather insulted by that. (*Stuart*)

Things are not always so bad, and the discrimination is not usually so blatant, but most antenatal classes are still not really geared to men's needs. This is especially true of hospital classes, although there are now some pilot schemes under way which seek to provide more directly for fathers' needs. I know of two British hospitals which are trying to set up fathers' support groups, although so far they have had a very limited response.

Even the private classes, whilst generally excellent and providing a much more relaxed and intimate atmosphere, tend to treat men as peripheral to the process; without any real needs of their own. This was brought home to me at a meeting I attended about fathers' antenatal needs. One of the men present was talking about his own experience of antenatal classes. He said that the teacher used to split the class into single sex groups for part of the time, something which he found very useful. Also present was a well-known and respected childbirth educator. She challenged him, saying that she didn't feel that men-only groups were a good idea. What had he been able to say in the male group that he couldn't say in the whole class?

He explained that during the pregnancy he had been quite worried about the amount of money his wife was spending on the forthcoming baby. He would not have brought this up in front of his wife and the other women in the group because he would not want to criticize her publicly. But it was good for him to be able to share his concern with other men — several of whom had similar worries. But, said the childbirth educator, hadn't he asked why his wife was spending so much money? Obviously it was a sign that she was unhappy and in need of more attention from him! Suddenly this father's perfectly understandable problem was devalued and he was made to feel guilty about a supposed lack of concern for his wife.

I protested about this, and the discussion got a little heated. One of the other antenatal teachers present tried to defuse the situation by suggesting that single-sex groups were not a good idea in antenatal classes anyway. Oh no, said the childbirth educator, single-sex women's groups are fine! This woman, a sensitive and impassioned champion of humane obstetrics in the labour room, had been in the forefront of advocating men's increasing involvement in parenting, yet even she seemed to see it as something of a threat.

A generation ago men were not usually directly involved in the months before birth; they watched their wives' pregnancies as spectators. Now many men participate in pregnancy; they share its stresses and strains and like the pregnant woman they become a little removed from normal life in preparation for their forthcoming change of status. The physical symptoms, changing attitudes, and other people's new reactions used to be reserved for women alone. It is a measure of men's increased commitment to involved fathering that they now share in this ritualized process.

5. The Birth Experience

Today it is the rule that a man should be present at the birth of his baby. Enormous pressure is put on the man who is reluctant — by both women and other men. Such is the power of the new orthodoxy. A generation ago it was very rare for a man to witness a birth, and even if he wanted to, permission was rarely given by the hospital authorities. Now in some places over 90% of men are there when their babies are born.[11]

Such a major change has many underlying causes, some more open and obvious than others. I think there have been three main pressures: from women, from the medical profession, and from men themselves. A closer look at the British figures shows an interesting trend. The number of women wanting their husbands to attend birth since World War II has increased faster than the number of men who actually attended. This suggests that men 'followed' women into the delivery room, accompanying them at first simply because their womenfolk have desired it.[12]

During this period we have also seen the removal of birth from the home into the hospital, which has had a large impact on the changing patterns of birth attendance. When birth was at home, in familiar surroundings, the family would be nearby, even if not actually present. The mother felt much more in control of the situation because she was on her own territory. In hospital things are different. The mother is isolated from family, friends and neighbourhood. The environment is strange, she does not make the rules, and she is under the control of others whom she may not know and may never have met before. In such circumstances it is not surprising that a woman should want a familiar face for moral support. The question is, why the father?

Traditionally, it is other women who provide companionship for women in labour. Some societies give this role to men, but the general rule is that a labour companion should be female — normally the woman's mother, although a sister, female friend or even mother-in-law might be also considered suitable. This used to be the case in the West also, but today it is rare for a woman to have a female labour companion. (In fact, it is my impression that there has been a slight increase in the number of female labour companions in the 1980s, but I don't know of any figures to confirm this.)

One reason for this may be found in our changing family and social patterns. Increasingly, people move away from the place where they were brought up, and as a result the old extended family ties have weakened, and new family patterns have grown up. In the traditional family the husband and wife have separate *networks* of friends and acquaintances. He will have mates from work, or his male relations, or people he meets down at the pub or bar, or fellow members of a sports club or other interest group. She will have her nearby neighbours, female family members — especially her mother and married sisters, other women she meets at work or in the shopping precinct, or at bingo or bridge.

The anthropologist Elizabeth Bott has suggested that a couple with closely knit networks — that is, when there are a lot of links between the individuals in a network — will be likely to have separate, traditional roles in marriage. They will tend to turn to their networks when they need help, rather than to each other. Couples with loosely knit networks are much more likely to do things together and to seek each other for comfort and support.

The trend, since the last War, has been towards the second kind of family structure. As people become more mobile in search of jobs and new opportunities, their traditional close knit networks break down. In their place there will be a much more loosely knit network, with a few friends from work, one or two neighbours, perhaps some people from the sports club and a few family members. Few of these people will know each other. In view of this it is hardly surprising that women should be asking their husbands to accompany them in labour. Who else could they turn to? It isn't just that other women are less available to act as labour companions, but also that we now believe that husband and wife should 'share' as many experiences as possible. As one woman said to me, "I told George that if he was keen enough to be there at the conception, he could be there at the birth as well".

The medical establishment at first refused to allow any labour companion into hospital. They said that he might endanger the birth process, or introduce infection into the labour room (medical objections to changes in practice are often couched in terms of sterility and infection). But gradually attitudes changed. Perhaps as a result of their wives' pressures some male doctors started being present at the birth of their own babies. Both they and their wives found it a positive experience, and there seemed to be no adverse side effects on mother or baby. Gradually they started to allow, and then encourage, men into the labour room.

In the United States the man who best exemplifies this trend is Dr Robert Bradley:

> Internationally known as the 'Father of Fathers', I was the first doctor ever to advocate the continual presence of the father in labor and birth, back in 1947. I chuckle over several Johnny-come lately methods with their claims that this began with them. (*Bradley*, p.31. This modest quote is from the third edition of the book, 1981.)

Bradley was a newly-qualified MD when his wife urged him to read Grantly Dick-Read's *Childbirth Without Fear*. His interest in natural childbirth was aroused and he started to teach and use it with his patients — who at that time were all unmarried mothers. It worked well, but his colleagues were sceptical. It wouldn't be any good with married women, they said; because they would still insist that labour was difficult and painful. Married women would have to put on a show of martyrdom for their husbands! So Bradley tried "the world's second most impossible obstetrical patients — married pregnant nurses". (The world's most impossible obstetric patients are, according to Bradley, "married pregnant female doctors".)

Despite the fact that their training tends to make them less compliant than ordinary patients, and their knowledge tends to make them worry about all the things which could go wrong, Bradley's methods were hugely successful. He remained throughout each labour, 'coaching' the woman and telling her what she ought to do to have a natural birth. According to Bradley, it was only when one newly delivered mother had thanked him most profusely, kissing him roundly in gratitude for his ministrations, that the scales dropped from his eyes.

> It struck me like a sledge hammer. What on earth was this lovely young woman kissing me for? Why was I the object of her gratitude as a labor coach while her young lover sat uselessly in the waiting room, fearful and anxious over his sweetheart's safety... (*Bradley*, pp.17-18)

So husbands were enrolled as labour coaches, and the movement into the delivery room began. Things went slowly at first. Bradley makes a distinction between 'delivery' which is the 'knock-'em-out, drag-'em-out' approach and 'birth' which is a natural event with no medication. It is apparently inappropriate for men to be present at delivery, but perfectly acceptable for them to be present at birth.

At first Bradley and those who thought like him were in a minority. Most obstetricians did not accept natural childbirth as either possible or desirable for 'civilized' Western women and continued to exclude men from the delivery. Even Bradley only allowed them in on his own terms:

> Husbands have no business being with their wives unless: (1) the wife has been trained how to perform in labor and has physically prepared her birth-giving muscles; (2) the husband has been prepared so that he understands how, why, and what his wife is doing, enabling him to coach, guide, and encourage her in her ennobling work. (*Bradley*, pp.20-21.)

Notice that the man is present as a 'husband', not a father. He has a job to do: to manage and guide his wife's labour — as a Robert Bradley substitute, perhaps. There is still no suggestion that a man should be present simply as a father in his own right. But gradually the climate of medical opinion loosened up and in the third edition of his book (1983) Bradley changed the word 'husband' to 'father'.

During the 1970s a succession of studies claimed that the presence of men in the delivery room could have three major benefits. Firstly, Bradley's claims were supported — the father *is* able to provide support and assistance to the mother; he is, in other words, able to *coach* her through her labour. Furthermore, the husband seemed to be more effective in this role than medical staff. Secondly, the presence of the father seemed to help the mother to relax more. This in turn both eased and speeded up the delivery. Mothers reported less pain and needed less medication when their partners were present. Thirdly, the presence of the father appeared to enhance the mother's appreciation of the birth experience. Fathers, it would seem, are good for mothers.[13] And of course, fathers may be useful as unpaid auxiliaries if there is a staff shortage — caused perhaps by an unexpectedly high number of deliveries at one time.

By the end of the seventies both mothers and medics were keen to have men present at birth. But what do men themselves want? What are their responses to this concerted pressure? Not surprisingly, reactions are mixed.

Some men simply don't want to be there at all. This reaction is becoming ever less common — or at least it is becoming less common to hear a man say that he doesn't want to be there. The 'uncommitted father', of course, will not want to be present. It's 'women's business' — nothing to do with him. Yet even he is less likely than before to express his sentiments too loudly. If he does he's in danger of being branded as an old-fashioned male chauvinist; a patriarchal dodo. He will be castigated by men and women alike, while his partner will be pitied and talked about behind her back. The new liberal orthodoxy demands that, whatever they feel, men must no longer talk of 'women's business' — everything must be shared.

The only person who might respectably share the uncommitted father's viewpoint — though not his views — is a radical feminist. She is happy to talk of 'women's business' and sees no harm at all in excluding men from large areas of her life. There are women who view any increase in men's interest in birth as just another attempt to increase male control over women and — especially in this case — over women's sexuality. A few men have been convinced by the feminist arguments, and are very reticent about any intrusion on 'female' areas of life.

But in truth a man does not have to be either callously uncaring or a radical feminist to wish to stay away from the delivery room. I received this letter some time ago in response to an article I wrote about the pressures on men to be 'good' fathers:

> We are expecting our first baby in a month's time and throughout my pregnancy my husband has given me all the support, both emotional and practical, that he can. He will not, however, be present at the birth because he has a tendency to become distressed and feel faint if he sees me in pain, bleeding, or being subjected to an injection. It is precisely because of this sensitivity towards me that he will absent himself at a time when he cannot help me and may indeed be a hindrance· to the hospital staff and cause me worry at a time when I have to concentrate on the job in hand.

The writer was concerned that her husband might be thought unfeeling, just because he was not going to be present at the birth. It may be rare for a man to faint in the delivery room, but it does happen occasionally. In this case both partners were aware of the risk, and acted in the way they thought best, out of concern, rather than lack of it.

Fear of fainting is not the only reason for staying away. A man may simply not wish to see his wife in what he (and she) may feel is a vulnerable and humiliating situation. Some men regard birth as a private matter, one which can be shared but not witnessed. Just because a function is natural does not mean that it is OK in company. Excreting is as natural a function as giving birth, but most couples don't feel any need to watch each other doing it.

I think that it is wrong for a couple to be pressured into performing together in the delivery room, just because some people think there should be no barriers to the sharing of experience between a couple. It seems to me that it is likely to do more harm than good to their relationship and their introduction to parenthood.

Most men today, whatever their private scruples, have decided to be present during labour, and probably during delivery as well. They say that they ought to be present, in order to 'help'. Or as one childbirth educator puts it:

> On the day of the labour and birth the father will be an integral part of the birth team, acting as liaison between the mother and the staff, and being the main support person and coach. (*Sundin*, p.3)

What this means in practice isn't always obvious. When babies were born in the movies, dad would pace in the hospital waiting room, chew his nails and smoke, or hand out large cigars. Eventually the cathartic moment would arrive when he was permitted a glance through a glass screen into the nursery, where a pretty young nurse held up a small shawl-wrapped bundle. Not much hint there about what it means to be an integral part of a birth team!

The movie dad had slightly more to do if his baby was born at home. He still paced endlessly of course, although now he waited at the bottom of the stairs. But he did seem to have one useful function to perform: he was required to find copious supplies of clean towels and boiling water. Some authorities suggest that this was just to keep him occupied and out of mischief, but the indefatiguable Robert Bradley has a different explanation.

According to Bradley, the towels and water were used to make hot salt compresses which were applied to the labouring woman's vagina and perineum. The compresses were alternated with applications of olive oil and manual massage of the vaginal opening to enlarge it. The result was that the skin lost its normal elasticity, making the birth easier. Unfortunately, according to Bradley, the tissues never regained their original shape or size.

The contemporary alternative to this treatment is *episiotomy*, which

Bradley, like many male obstetricians, enthusiastically espouses. An episiotomy is a small cut made in the perineum, the skin between vagina and anus, which makes delivery easier. It is a controversial operation, almost routine in America, but rare in some other developed countries. Its opponents say that it is seldom necessary, and is only performed because the delivering obstetrician or midwife is too eager to 'get the baby out' instead of waiting a little longer and aiding the natural rhythms of the body.

I don't want to discuss the pros and cons of episiotomy here, but I do want to stress that birth is not simply — or even primarily — a medical event. It does not take place in a vacuum, but reflects social values and ideologies. The things that are done and the experiences which are encouraged are themselves related to our views of parenthood. In chapter seven I will take a closer look at the ritual and symbolic aspects of birth; here I just want to point out that most of what we do could be done differently. Our ideas of the proper way to conduct a birth must be seen in the wider context of social and political beliefs and experiences.

But if society has decreed that the obstetrician's cut should take over from the father's kettles of boiling water, just what is the attendant father to do now? What does 'coaching' involve? For Bradley it starts well before birth, and includes such vital activities as squatting, relaxation, and 'pelvic rocks'. It is not the husband who has to perform these antics, but it is his job to ensure that his wife does them.

> It doesn't matter how late it is or how tired she may claim to be; don't let her in bed with you until she does her pelvic rocking! (*Bradley*, p.100)

At the birth itself the husband's role is even more demanding. For instance, the Australian author quoted earlier lists a dozen things the father will be responsible for, including staying with the mother at all times, reminding her to empty her bladder at regular intervals, showing pride in her, keeping a written log of the labour, and ensuring good rapport with the birth team, with tact, good humour and respect.

But perhaps the most important of the father's responsibilities, and the one that most clearly summarizes his role, is "Providing appropriate physical and emotional support, being sensitive to her changing needs throughout the varying phases of labour". This is reinforced with a list of twenty-one further specific suggestions to do with relaxation, breathing, massage and encouragement. Finally the father is reminded that during delivery itself, "Your partner will no doubt have an earthy and instinctive involvement in this fantastic phase of labour. Don't be embarrassed, allow her to be herself and birth the baby in her own way." (*Sundin*, pp.3-6)

The father who goes to the birth because he wants to help thus finds that there are two rather conflicting sets of expectations forced upon him. He must in some way 'coach'; be in charge of the labour, and he must also be clear that he is quite subordinate to the needs and dictates of his partner. Despite this apparent contradiction, most men seem reasonably satisfied with their role. A survey done at the West London Hospital in the UK asked 730 men how they thought they had contributed to their partner's labour. Easily the most common response was that they had helped to sustain her morale. Providing physical comfort and help with her breathing exercises during labour also figured strongly.[14]

The role of labour companion is a hard one for a father to play. Ideally it requires selflessness and detatchment — hardly the easiest qualities to cultivate while your partner is in distress and your baby is being born. The experience of seeing a beloved in pain is one which makes a deep impression on many men:

> I felt really awful about it, totally helpless you know, because there was nothing you could do. We went through all the exercises and things like that, but then it got to the point where even that wasn't helping, she just couldn't use it. It was just that the pain just totally took over everything and that was really hard for me to take as well. (*Andy*)

I don't want to deny the pain of labour or pretend that it's the men who really suffer, but it is important to recognize that labour is often difficult for men too. Men are used to *doing*; many find it hard simply to accept a difficult situation. The woman's pain can become the man's guilt. It was through his action that she became pregnant (no matter that they both wanted it), and now she suffers while he is powerless to do anything about it.

The problem of 'doing' is one which crops up a lot in the context of fatherhood. In the labour room there is little to do — especially for the man who feels that the paternalistic approach of Bradley and his followers is demeaning to women. The role of a labour companion, as opposed to a labour coach, is to support, not to direct. It is the woman who is giving birth; it is she who is experiencing the agony and ecstasy. The labour companion is there to give help and support; which often involves little more than simply being there.

I have often heard couples talking about their birth experiences. "I couldn't have managed without him," she says, "he made all the difference." "But I didn't do anything" he protests. And in truth there is little you can do. A bit of massage, cooling her down with a damp sponge when appropriate, and helping her to remember how to do her breathing.

I was a complete failure at the latter — and it felt like failure, too. I've never been good at exams; I always thought I'd revised properly and knew the subject but when I got the paper in front of me I realized that I didn't really know it at all. It was the same in labour. I thought I knew all about the different kinds of breathing recommended by the antenatal teacher, but when it came to the crunch I forgot the lot! So I wasn't much help there. The only thing which came to my aid was the wonderful monitoring machine.

Like most men, I find machines reasonably accessible. So the fetal monitor, showing the baby's heart beat and the build up of contractions provided almost endless fascination. More to the point, it was possible to see the start of a contraction building up before Shirley was able to feel it. This meant that I could warn her of the impending pain, and thus she was able to cope with it a bit better. It seemed like a positive contribution to the proceedings, and it is one which many other men have also discovered. Women are not always so keen; I've often heard them moan that their husbands paid more attention to the machines than to them.

Unfortunately there is a lot of unnecessary monitoring, and it can have some serious adverse consequences for mother and baby. Fetal monitoring usually restricts mobility, preventing the mother from moving around during the first stage of labour. Since walking about helps the progress of labour and makes it less painful, anything which prevents it is to be discouraged. It is therefore a pity that the fetal monitor should be so attractive to those men who feel the need to justify their existence in the delivery room. So long as men are told that their primary reason for being there is to 'help' they will have to try to find ways of helping, even if those ways are counterproductive to the progress of labour.

While most men still see their main role as that of helper, a change is gradually occurring. Fewer men are now willing or able to act *only* as a labour companion. She is becoming a mother, but he is becoming a father, and so has a need to become part of the birth experience in his own right. This is a change which has not really been assimilated by the obstetric establishment. Hospitals and women are still keen, by and large, to have men as labour companions. Any other involvement is secondary and may be viewed with either pleasure (most women) or displeasure (most hospitals). But increasingly, men are telling each other that it is the emotional experience which counts. One recent book for fathers, generally excellent, tells us that:

> During your partner's labour you'll probably feel a wide range of emotions. You'll feel terrified, ecstatic, exhausted; but you won't be bored, even if you decide that you don't want to be present. (*Bradman*, p.130)

I think that it is dangerous and misleading to try to lay down appropriate emotional behaviour for a man in the delivery room. Because many men *are* bored — especially during a long first stage when there seems to be little progress.

> It was a nice experience, that I wouldn't have missed, but if I hadn't been there with a camera in my hand taking photographs of the baby coming out and that, I would have felt as though I was just a bystander — anybody could have been there other than me. (*Ian*)

There is sometimes a suggestion — usually left unvoiced — that a man who doesn't react emotionally to the birth is not going to be very concerned about his children. Interestingly, two of the men I know who were least impressed by the birth experience are both looking after their children full time while their wives work. They both experience the normal frustrations and aggravations of full-time parenthood, but neither could be described as uninvolved or unconcerned — quite the reverse.

However it is true that *most* men do find the experience of birth quite overwhelming, and almost impossible to describe. There is something both touching and amusing in hearing a new father tell others of his birth. When he gets to the delivery itself, he will almost always use broken phrases and commonplace clichés:

> It's a fantastic experience and...and they are so aware when they come out. They look at you like, like,... well as though you're the first thing they've ever seen and...it's a fantastic feeling...yeah...it's worth it for that... (*John*).

But the clichés don't matter. Everyone knows what he means, and they smile and nod benignly, remembering the moment for themselves.

Everyone is unprepared for the experience of birth and no-one can really describe it properly for others, just because it is so personal. Sheila Kitzinger has repeatedly described giving birth as a psychosexual experience for a woman, and it occurs to me that the analogy may also be illuminating for some men. It seems to provide a way of describing the development of a man's involvement in labour too.

We often forget how physical a birth can be. What is a man's job as labour companion? It is to massage, cuddle, console, caress, and stroke his partner. In public. For hour after hour. And she, hardly dressed at all. That *her* involvement is direct and physical, no-one can doubt. His may not be so direct, but it need be no less physical.

Some couples — particularly if their antenatal classes have not prepared them to be so intimate in public — may find it hard to perform. They may even be so embarrassed that he doesn't attend at all. But most manage to shut out the spectators — who seem to fade into the background as absorption in the matter at hand gets more intense.

I never thought of birth as a sexual event when I was in the delivery room, but looking back it seems as good a way of portraying the essence of it as any other. Perhaps one reason why the moment so overwhelms and surprises us is that it is so much like an orgasm. Not in an obviously physical sense, but more in the release of tension; in the feeling of relief and joy that the long-awaited consumation has occurred. Yet there was never an orgasm like this. For a start, the build up takes so long. You prepare for nine months until the time arrives. And then it starts, gently at first, but with ever increasing intensity as time goes on; two hours, five hours, ten hours, fifteen hours, maybe even more. Not even the supermen of the *Kama Sutra* can match this! Perhaps this is why men feel so let down, so bitter, if they are thrown out of the delivery room before the birth is complete. It is the frustration and sense of incompleteness which accompanies *coitus interruptus*.

After such a build up, the birth itself is almost unbearable. Time stretches and contracts. It seems to take for ever, yet happens in a flash. And it isn't a release at all, just a heightening of already impossible tension. The senses are all working overtime, focused down on the important part of the universe. Every nuance of the moment comes straight through. The top of the head appears, then retracts. "I can see the head" you say, clasping her hand desperately, hanging on to reality for all you're worth.

Then suddenly it's out. Release begins, but immediately is stifled. The student stiffens. The midwife moves smoothly towards her. "Hold it there" she says. Something is wrong. The cord is wrapped twice round the baby's neck. It seemed impossible to get any more involved or anxious, but now you know differently. Time stops as you watch fascinated, then before you can panic, the cord is cut. They relax. You start to relax. The rest of the baby — "A boy!" you cry, anxious to be the first to say it — slips out so sensuously that you can almost feel it. Quickly they weigh him, check him, evaluate him. Is he alright? "Has he got everything? Has he got two...?" And he has.

Now there is time to breathe again; now it is possible to let go. And come down, down, down... Sobbing, gasping, laughing, high and low all at once. And together; it is not just one alone, but the two — no, now you are three. It took so long to come, this orgasm of parenthood, but now that it has arrived it ought to go on for ever. The outside world won't let it of course. There are routines, procedures, examinations. They always intrude too soon, and then the moment is over. It stays with you though, and later on you too may try to explain it in your own incoherent way. Just make sure you explain it to someone who's already been through it — otherwise you'll get some very funny looks!

Is *this*, then, the point of it all? Are we there just for that moment? Perhaps all of the coaching and companionship is just foreplay for this climax of new life? I think I've noticed a change over the last few years. Men used to tell other men to be present at birth for their wives' sake. Now, more often, they mention the wonderful experience. It's not a question of one or the other, but there has been a serious shift in emphasis and many hospitals are finding it difficult to cope with.

It is well known that hospitals are based on hierarchies of power with doctors at the top, nurses in the middle and patients at the bottom. In the delivery room, the father comes even lower still. As long as he is prepared to stay there, being a labour companion and generally knowing his place then there is a reasonable chance that his presence will be tolerated.

When, in 1973, I wanted to be present for the birth of our first child, hospitals were still uncertain about the idea. I had to sign a form absolving the hospital of any responsibility and agreeing to do whatever they told me. I was made to leave the room whenever Shirley had to be examined and in the end I was excluded from the delivery because the baby was delivered by a Ventouse (vacuum extraction). The possibility that I might faint was raised by the staff more than once, and it was very clear that I was there simply as a spectator, someone who had no positive role to perform and who really had little business to be present.

Things have changed since then. But the committed father, the man who wants the birth of his child to be a special event for himself as well as his partner, still faces an uphill struggle before his needs and desires will be fully met. The more he asks for, the greater the resistance. Yet in the end, if his demands are moderate and considerate he will succeed. In a real sense fatherhood begins at birth. The experience of birth can be a powerful expression of the values of parenthood. If a man tries to take an active and responsible part in the birth of his child, is he not more likely to do the same throughout the rest of his life? But if he is simply a subordinate, subservient both to the medical hierachy and to his wife will he not be likely to continue his shadowy role, always taking second place?

Birth both expresses and confirms our hopes and goals for parenthood. To this extent it is possible to think of it as a ritual event, full of meaning and social significance. The fact that fathers now participate with increasing vigour in the birth process is itself a powerful symbolic statement about the importance of establishing the ties of fatherhood.

6. How To Become a Father

With the birth of the baby comes the birth of fatherhood. The new father can now leave behind the shifting sands and uncertainties of pregnancy, secure in the knowledge that at last his status is secure. We may not know how to behave towards, or even describe, a pregnant man, but surely everybody agrees on what it is to be a father?

In fact things are not so simple. Anthropologists have discovered that fatherhood is actually such a slippery and flexible concept that *anybody* can become a father, in one culture or another; child or adult, male or female, living or dead!

So in this chapter I want to take a break from the small-scale and introverted world of the delivery room, to ask a simple question, "What is a father?" The answer you get depends on who you ask. In order to explore it, I want to look at the meaning of fatherhood in a variety of cultures, ranging from ancient Israel to twentieth century Africa and the Pacific Islands. But although this digression will take us all round the world, it is crucial to the flow of the book, for it will bring us back to the very labour ward we have just left.

First, consider the following story from the Bible about Judah and his three sons Er, Onan, and Shelah:

> Judah found a wife for his eldest son, Er; her name was Tamar. But Judah's eldest son Er was wicked in the LORD's sight, and the LORD took his life. Then Judah told Onan to sleep with his brother's wife, to do his duty as the husband's brother and raise up issue for his brother. But Onan knew that the issue would not be his; so whenever he slept with his brother's wife, he spilled his seed on the ground so

as not to raise up issue for his brother. What he did was wicked in the LORD's sight, and the LORD took his life. (Genesis 38:6-10 *New English Bible*)

The meaning of this story is hard to grasp at first. Clearly Onan did something wrong; but what? Many commentators have thought that this passage means that Onan was masturbating, and that this was his sin. The word onanism has even passed into the language as a synonym for masturbation — "self-pollution" as Chambers called it 250 years ago. In fact, rather than masturbating, Onan was probably withdrawing before ejaculation — *coitus interruptus.* Yet it was not this in itself which caused God's wrath. The real issue was the lack of issue.

The point is that Onan's brother, Er, had died without becoming a father; he had no-one to remember his name or carry on his line. After Er's death it became Onan's duty to get Tamar pregnant so that she could have children who would be Er's rightful and legitimate heirs. Onan refused because he wanted the children to be his and not his brother's.

It is hard to see the true meaning of this unless we can throw off our traditional Western ways of looking at fatherhood. The point here is that even though Er was dead he could still have become a father if Onan had been willing to donate his seed for the purpose.

Customs like this are still practised today and make very good sense in the cultures where they are found. In order for us to understand them it is necessary to split our ideas of fatherhood in two. We must distinguish between the man who provides the seed; whose biological action causes the child to be conceived, and the man who is legally recognized as the father of the child; who will bring up the child and whose name and property the child will inherit.

The physical father is called the *genitor*, the legal father the *pater*. We are accustomed to assume that the two roles should be performed by one and the same person, but many societies see no reason why this should be so. For instance, if we look at the Bible story in these terms we can see that Onan was supposed to be the genitor while Er was supposed to be the pater — even though he was dead!

Our knowledge of the social organization of the ancient Israelites is limited, but similar customs are still practised in many parts of the world. To shed more light on the notion that a man might become a father after he is dead, consider the Nuer of East Africa.

The Nuer are a group of people who live in the Southern Sudan. They are cattle herders, who move between summer and winter pastures many miles apart. They have no central government, no chiefs, nor even tribal councils to keep order. Rather, the extended family provides the main way of organizing society. The Nuer are *patrilineal*: family membership is counted in the male line only. Children belong to the family, or *lineage*, of their father. Marriage between members of the same lineage is forbidden, so a man's wives (a Nuer man may have more than one wife) must inevitably come from a different lineage. Consequently, daughters move out to become the wives of men from other lineages, and so are lost to the family of their father.

An in-marrying wife joins the family of her husband and becomes equivalent to one of his kinswomen. Thus it is only sons who are able to carry on the family line. It is very important to a man that his name be continued through his male children. If he dies without a son to remember him, it is believed that his spirit will be unable to rest easily, and may return to cause sickness and trouble amongst his surviving relatives.

Marriage among the Nuer is a long process, consisting of a series of rituals, and payments of cattle. The Nuer are one of many societies which practice *bridewealth*, in which the groom and his family give cattle, or other valuables, to the bride's family to compensate them for the loss of their daughter and any children she may subsequently bear (which will, of course, belong to the groom's lineage). Bridewealth has sometimes been thought of as a kind of slavery, where a man 'buys' his wife from her father or uncle. It is often more accurate to look on it as a form of compensation for the loss of a daughter. In any case, the cattle are rarely kept, but usually have to be passed on to another family so that the bride's brothers will themselves be able to marry and have children to continue their lineage.

When the final payment of marriage cattle has been made, and the various ceremonies performed, the groom is allowed to consummate the marriage. From this time on he will be the legal father of any child which his bride might bear. If she turns out to be barren, the marriage will be called off, and the bridewealth cattle will have to be returned by her parents.

It is hard to get enough cattle to pay bridewealth and many men die without having a chance to marry. This is a disaster for the man, and for his family, since he will have no sons to remember him or appease his spirit. So, despite the fact of his death, he *will* get married. The usual pattern is that one of his younger brothers will go through the marriage ceremonies on the dead man's behalf. The younger brother will consummate the marriage and will help bring up the children, but it is the dead man who will be considered the legal father of the children and it is *his* name they will remember. The dead man is pater, his younger brother is genitor; and it is the pater who is more important for the Nuer.

In a similar way, if a man marries, but dies before having any sons, it is the duty of one of his close kinsmen — usually a younger brother — to take the widow into his home and raise sons for the dead man by her. The Nuer consider that the widow is still the wife of the dead man, not of the relative who now looks after her, and it is the dead man who will be father to any children born as a result of the new arrangements.

This custom, of raising sons to a dead man, is known as the *levirate* and is found in many societies in Africa. It explains why Onan in the Bible story was so upset and why his crime was considered so bad. He wanted sons who would remember *his* name, whereas any sons which Tamar bore would be for Er, not for him. Onan tried to opt out of his responsibilities (and perhaps imply that Tamar was barren and should be returned to her family) but he was punished for his selfishness towards his elder brother.

The Bangwa, who live in the Cameroon in West Africa, have a more complex political system than the Nuer, with a 'royalty' of chiefs and subchiefs much like a medieval system of princes and noblemen. They are farmers and traders and they count kinship ties through both male and female parents rather than just the male line as the Nuer do. The Bangwa say that women provide the red blood (menstrual blood) and men provide the white blood (semen) when a child is made. During the first two months of pregnancy the womb shakes and mixes up these two bloods, and so both parents have a share in the child. Political allegiances depend on male links, while the closest family groups are held together by female links.

Powerful Bangwa men marry many wives; this becomes a sign of their prestige and wealth. A famous chief, Asunganyi, who died in 1952 was said to have had over a hundred wives. The Bangwa differ from the Nuer in that they practice *widow inheritance*. When a man dies his wives will be inherited by his heirs, along with his property. The father of any children subsequently borne by any of these women will not be the dead husband, as in the Nuer case, but the person inheriting the wives — even if he should only be a baby of a few months old! Obviously in such a case he will not be able to be the biological father, and his trustees will probably fulfill this function for him until he comes of age. But the child will be the legal father of any children born.

A man's heir is usually, but not necessarily, another man. Robert Brain, the anthropologist who lived with the Bangwa for two years, reports that the chief's sister, Mafwankeng, inherited two of her father's wives. She decided to give one out in marriage and to keep the other as her own wife.

Subsequently she married a young girl as a second wife. Each of her wives has a lover who visits her in secret. His identity should be known to no-one but the 'husband' and the midwife who delivers any children of the union. The children will inherit from their female father just as if she were male, and she will take the father's share of any bridewealth paid for her daughters. This kind of marriage is not common among the Bangwa, being mainly reserved to wealthy and powerful noblewomen, but it is not considered strange or in any way deviant. It fits perfectly well into the logic of Bangwa fatherhood, which is that a father is the person who has certain legal rights and duties concerning the child.

Anthropology, the study of how different societies are organized, is a fascinating subject in its own right. It allows us to acquire knowledge about the ways in which different people behave: to look at some of the marvellous and wonderful things human beings do, and to try to make sense of people's behaviour. Knowledge for itself is valuable, but anthropology can go further. The results of such study can be used as a mirror to let us look at ourselves and our behaviour in a new light. We tend to think that our own ways are not just the best, but the *only* ways to do things. Looking at others shows us that this is not so. Reflection such as this can be particularly useful when, as now, the institution of fatherhood is in a state of flux.

Until recently it would probably have been true to say that ghost fathers or female fathers were quite without precedent or analogy in our society. Today, in a climate of rapidly changing attitudes towards paternity, this is no longer true. It is now possible in Western society for a man to become a father after his death — a ghost father. There have been several instances when a man, learning that he has contracted a fatal disease such as cancer, has deliberately arranged for samples of his semen to be kept in a sperm bank, so that his wife may bear his children by artificial insemination after his death.

This is still a rather new idea to most of us, and we are not entirely sure how to deal with it, but it seems that most people would be happy to treat this dead man as the legitimate father of any such children born after his death. It is not clear whether this is because it was his sperm which caused conception, or because of his past relationship with the mother and her desire to have his children. I think that the sperm are the key. If the mother were to be artificially inseminated by an unknown donor after her husband's death, most people would be rather doubtful about accepting any claim that real father of the child was the dead husband. And if she had a casual affair in order to become pregnant, it is even more unlikely that her claim would be accepted.

Similarly, it is possible to find an analogy to female fatherhood. The Summer 1984 edition of the *Men's Anti-Sexist Newsletter* carried the following advertisement: "Donors wanted for feminist self-insemination group. Write to Box 3,..." While the women of the self-insemination group would probably repudiate the whole notion of fatherhood (see also chapter 11), there might be a sense in which they could be said to be practising female fatherhood — especially given the fact that we are no longer sure what a father is, or how he (or she?) is supposed to behave. Our very definitions of fatherhood, once so firm and obvious, are now under fire, and looking at the way other peoples think behave and feel can help us to straighten out our own thinking.

Fatherhood is never natural or obvious. I believe, like just about everyone in my culture, that babies are produced by sexual intercourse — though I must admit that I can't actually prove it. In fact, although I believe that intercourse is necessary for conception, I also know that not every act of intercourse causes conception. Further, I have absolutely no way of telling if or when a specific sexual act will produce conception.

Despite these serious gaps in my knowledge, I believe that I am the biological father of three children: Mark, Adam and Rebecca. Again, I have no certain proof of this. I do know for a fact that Shirley, my wife, has given birth to three children and I am sure that I played a significant part in their conception.

I also know that it is possible to establish with a high degree of probability whether or not a man is genetically linked with his children. But I have had no such tests — nor do I feel any need for them because my cultural 'knowledge' (belief) is strong enough to sustain me. Although I am able to accept intellectually that there is little genuine evidence for my belief in my own paternity, I have no real doubts about it.

While we believe, despite the rather flimsy evidence available to most of us, that there is a link between intercourse and conception, this is not true of everyone. There are peoples, in Australia and the Pacific Islands who until recently denied that such a link exists.[15] Most of the controversy has centred round the reported beliefs of people from the Trobriand Islands. The Trobriand Islanders are a fishing and gardening people who live on a coral archipelago lying to the north-east of Papua New Guinea. Like the Nuer they reckon descent through one parent only — but in their case, through the mother rather than the father. In this kind of system — a *matrilineal* system — a child will be a member or his or her mother's family (lineage) rather than the father's family. Matrilineal societies are found throughout the world, although they are not as common as patrilineal societies such as the Nuer. Some feminist writers have suggested that in a matrilineal society the mother is the head of the family. In fact, this is not the case.

In the Trobriand Islands, as in most societies, property and power are, in general, held by men. This means that a man's heir is not his own son (who is not a member of his lineage) but his *sister's* son. Or, to look at it from the other end, the family head from whom a man will inherit from is not his father or his mother, but his mother's brother. In a matrilineal society a man's descendants are not his own children, but his sister's, and the Trobriand beliefs about conception help to confirm and explain this fact.

According to Bronislaw Malinowski, who spent most of the First World War there, the Trobriand Islanders deny that men have any part to play in the conception of children. Instead, they maintain that a baby is born because a 'spirit child' has entered the woman. When a person dies, his or her spirit (*baloma*) goes to the mythical island of Tuma where it continues its existence in a happy after-life. Eventually it will get tired of this life and decide to be re-incarnated. The baloma will turn itself into a little spirit child and make its way back to the Trobriand Islands. There he or she will enter the body of a suitable woman.

There are two native theories about conception. Some people say that the spirit child enters through the mother's head, others say that it does so through her vagina. The mother's blood helps to nourish and build up the spirit child, which is why menstruation stops during pregnancy. Although the Trobriand Islanders deny that intercourse has anything to do with actually making babies, it is accepted that it has some part to play in the process. Unless a woman is 'opened up' by intercourse, she will be unable to conceive; the spirit will be unable to enter her.

A different set of beliefs about spirit children and conception can be found among the Orokaiva of Papua New Guinea. Erik Schwimmer reports that male children are said to be born as the result of sexual intercourse *and* the entry of a spirit child, whereas female children are born just as a result of the spirit child entering the mother. In the former case, the male spirit child may either have entered the father first and thence from him into the mother, or it may have entered the mother directly.

Orokaiva naming customs are consistent with these beliefs. A girl child is always named by the mother or her relatives, while a boy child may be named by either paternal or maternal relatives. Nevertheless, the mother's husband — provided he has paid the full bridewealth — will be pater to both girls and boys, although genitor to the boys only. This theory allows the Orokaiva to account for the differences between the sexes. Men differ from women by having a special quality (*ivo*) which is transmitted to male children by the 'male blood' (semen) when it is transferred to the mother during intercourse.

In other societies the link between paternity and intercourse is clear and unequivocal. The Kamano who live in the New Guinea highlands hold that fatherhood is created by one act of intercourse, demonstrated by the failure of the woman's period, and is unaffected by any subsequent sexual relationship that the woman might have either with the father or with anyone else. The biological link is itself sufficient to make a man a father, and this is not affected by whether he is married to the mother of the child.

Adultery seems to be common and this can confuse the issue. If a woman has intercourse with two or more men in the month before her periods stop, the most vigorous man, or the one who has already demonstrated the greatest fertility by siring other children, will be taken to be the father. If all other things are equal, then the husband of the woman will be presumed to be the father. However, no amount of love and attention can cancel or override the physical link between natural father and son. Elizabeth Mandeville tells of one old man who learned, during a quarrel, that he was not the son of his mother's husband, but of her lover. Immediately he left his home and land and went to live in the village of his biological father — and this despite the fact that Kamano villages are very insular and often hostile to one another.

Where do we, of the developed West, stand? How do we define fatherhood? At first sight we appear to be like the Kamano, stressing the biological link to the exclusion of all else. Like most societies we do distinguish between pater and genitor, but for us it is the genitor who seems to be most important. One casual act of intercourse is enough to make a man (genitor) the 'real' father of a child — even if he has no more contact with the mother, and even if another man (pater) acts as father; caring, loving and nurturing that child for many years. Put in this way it may not seem right; surely fatherhood means more than casual copulation? It is a question which has caused adoptive parents much anguish for many years. But there are signs that things are slowly changing.

Although we express the basis of fatherhood in purely biological terms, in practice this has always been a rather uncertain means of definition. The trouble is that you can't usually tell if a particular child is yours or somebody else's. This uncertainty can be seen in the jokes frequently made about the new baby looking like the postman or the father's best friend. It is often the new father himself who will make such jokes, perhaps to seek reassurance from others. And he often gets it. According to one study people are much more likely to comment on resemblances between father and child than between mother and child — whether or not they actually look alike. The mother is more likely than anyone to make such comments.[16]

Although we usually regard biology as providing the symbolic basis for fatherhood, in practice we need something a little more certain. So, like the Kamano, we assume that, unless there is good evidence to the contrary, it is the mother's husband who must be the father of the child. In this sense the father's relationship with his children is not a direct one, but is mediated through their mother. As long as marriage is universal and stable, this principle works quite well. But if the marriage pattern changes, fatherhood is one of the first things to suffer.

We can see this in two ways. Firstly, in English law at least, a man has no rights over his illegitimate child. Even if everyone admits that he is the biological father he has no responsibility in law for the child unless he is married to the child's mother. He has to apply for a court order before he can have any rights of access or custody. The child's mother has these rights automatically. The British Law Commission advocated in 1979 that the status of illegitimacy should be abolished and, in consequence, that all fathers should be treated in the same way regardless of whether they are married to the child's mother. So far no action has been taken on this and it seems as if the proposal is too far ahead of public opinion to stand much chance of being accepted just yet.

The father of an illegitimate child is called a *putative* father, and the only other way he can have a legitimate link with his child (apart from adopting her or marrying the mother) is to co-operate with the child's mother in getting an affiliation order. This is a legal order stating that a named man is the father of a single woman's child (she may not apply if she is married). It is generally used by a woman so that a court will make a maintainance order against the man to force him to support the child. As such it is designed to help her when the man is unwilling to accept at least the financial responsibilities of fatherhood. Despite this rather unsavoury aspect to it, some men encourage such court proceedings.

Brian is the father of a six year old daughter. He is not married to her mother, Jean, who lives in a city several hundred miles away, but they remain friends and he sees them both regularly. Brian's fatherhood means a lot to him and his separation from his daughter is a source of regret. He was present at her birth and is very keen to be part of her life. Jill and Brian have never disagreed about access or the amount of maintainance that he should pay to her, so there hasn't been any practical need for court action. Nevertheless, Brian told me that he encouraged Jill to apply for an affiliation order because it was the only way that his fatherhood could be legally and publicly acknowledged.

The importance of marriage to fatherhood can also be seen when marriage fails. A father still has very little chance of being awarded custody of his children. Unless a woman has deserted her children, or can be shown to be grossly unfit to have care and control of them, she will nearly always be given custody by the courts. Groups of divorced fathers, such as 'Fathers United for Equal Justice' in the US or 'Families Need Fathers' in the UK, have banded together to try change things. They try to improve their rights: by attempting, for instance, to make sure that the parent without custody will still have his voice heard by the child's school, and also by pressing for changes in the law and in the way custody is awarded.

There is another way in which changing marriage patterns are forcing us to re-examine our ideas of fatherhood. Charlie married Maureen fourteen years ago. She had two small children from her first marriage, the youngest under one year old when she met Charlie. Her first husband emigrated soon after her divorce and neither she nor the children have heard from him since. Charlie loves Emma and Jane and they love him and always call him 'Dad'. If biology is the sole basis of fatherhood then Charlie is not their 'real' father, but they will not accept that. The man who sired them is a shadowy figure who has no real place in their lives. Thousands of men are in the same position as Charlie. When they have cared and loved and wept and laughed with their step-children, sometimes for many years, it seems impossible to deny that they are true fathers. Biology may matter, but is it more important than love?

Artificial insemination by donor (AID) removes yet another foundation stone from the dominance of the physical father. More and more couples, usually happily married, are resorting to AID if the husband turns out to be infertile or in some way unable to produce children. Norman had custody of the three daughters from his first marriage. A few months before his first wife left him, she persuaded him to have a vasectomy. When he met Jean and they decided to get married, they were both aware that they would be unable to have any children of their own. Nevertheless, after a couple of years Jean realized that she did want a child of their own, and in particular that she wanted to go through the experience of pregnancy and birth.

Artificial insemination by donor seemed to be the only option to allow this. The three girls would be biologically related to Norman but not to Jean, while the new baby would be biologically related to Jean but not Norman. Nevertheless they were convinced that this would make little difference and that they would both be true parents to all the children.

In due course Jill became pregnant and gave birth to a little son. Norman was present at the birth and was as proud and excited as any biological father. His name is on the birth certificate as the father, even though in English law an AID child is illegitimate and the birth entry should read "father not known", or else be left blank.[17]

Many couples today live together and only marry when they want to have children. Yet in the UK one marriage in three ends in divorce. In the US the figure is even higher. Men are beginning to realize that neither a biological link nor the marriage tie may be enough to create a deep and lasting relationship with their children. When marriage was secure many men tended to take their fatherhood for granted; now it is seen as something which needs to be worked at.

What we are seeing now is an upsurge of interest in fathering at the same time as there is an apparent breakdown of the family. Some writers see this as something of a paradox, but I think the two are causally connected. Much of the new interest and concern about fathering can be traced directly to this new family uncertainty. In the last chapter I discussed some of the reasons for men's arrival in the delivery room. At the end of the chapter I hinted at another — one of the most potent: *a man wants to be present at the birth of his child because it is a ritual declaration of his paternity.*

In 1968 Mary Douglas wrote an article about the *couvade* rituals which men in some societies undergo while their wives are giving birth. She claims that such rituals are to be found in societies where the marriage tie is weak, or is not strongly institutionalized. In societies where there is a transfer of bridewealth there will be little concern about paternity because the bridewealth itself is sufficient to create paternity. But in other societies — including ours — things are different. Mary Douglas wrote:

> Already one notices a new emphasis on the father's role in the lying-in of the mother, and a new responsibility for the mental health of his children, an emphasis which I would expect to be increasing with the greater ease of divorce. (p.67)

It is nearly twenty years since that prediction was made and it seems to have been spectacularly accurate.

Other studies have confirmed and extended this insight. Karen &

Jeffrey Paige have looked at the strength of support a man gets during his life from his relatives, particularly his brothers. Couvade rituals are most common in societies where a man has little support from his relatives, and has to establish his paternity claims by gathering support from society at large. The rituals may be quite disruptive to others because the man won't hunt or work in the fields, or perhaps will only eat certain foods or needs other special consideration. If people encourage him, despite the inconvenience to themselves, it is a strong sign that they accept his paternity. Further, his own acceptance of the inconvenience may help to convince others that his claim is justified.

The converse can also be true: a man may fail to perform couvade rituals because he refuses to accept paternity. Allan Holmberg gives an example of this among the Sirionó of Bolivia. A man went hunting during his wife's delivery although it was his duty to cut the cord. She waited all day with the baby still attached to the placenta. When the husband returned he was eventually persuaded to cut the cord, but he still insisted that the child was not his.

Being present at birth is only one aspect of couvade ritual and is actually rather uncommon when looked at in global terms. Birth is usually considered to be women's work and men are either excluded or uninterested. But in our society birth is the most heavily ritualized activity to do with parenthood, as we will see in the next chapter, and it is this which makes it central to men's attempt to demonstrate paternity.

Yet it is true that most parents are largely unaware of its ritual aspects. When, in 1972, I wanted to be present at Mark's birth I was not aware of any outside pressures — either social or ritual. It was simply something I wanted to do both for myself and for Shirley. Nor was I conscious of any uncertainty about my own marriage or forthcoming paternity. But there was no doubt that it did proclaim my fatherhood to the world and I did not mind that a bit. Being Mark's mother's husband was not enough for me, and my presence at the birth was a symbolic statement of that fact.

7. Passage to Parenthood

Our society is full of rituals. Some mark large scale events like a royal wedding or the inauguration of a president. Others are more commonplace, such as church services or the changing of the guard at Buckingham Palace. But these all have one thing in common: they are formal rituals, for public consumption, and teams of experts have carefully worked out their form. But there are other rituals too; which are less public and less self-consciously created. Because of this there is a tendency not to recognize them as rituals at all.

It is hard to define *ritual* to everyone's satisfaction. But most experts agree that rituals contain stylized elements and operations which are performed because they have symbolic meaning or help the ritual to develop. They are not carried out principally in order to produce some material effect. Many rituals are repetitive and predictable, at least in their broad outlines.

One interesting thing about Western rituals is that many of them are not actually recognized as being rituals by those involved in them. Indeed, the people responsible for arranging and performing the events may often strenuously deny the claim. But the fact remains that these events are structured in the same ways and contain the same elements as other, more obvious, rituals and it seems sensible to treat the two in the same way.

Labelling a procedure as 'ritual' is not a criticism. There is a belief in some parts of our society that rituals are pointless; a meaningless expression of old-fashioned superstition. This is not generally so. Rituals can be very helpful to us all — especially in situations of uncertainty, or change of social role.

Taken as a whole, modern obstetric procedures contain a mix of the ritual and the medical. Some of the procedures may be of little or no ritual consequence, but are medically important — taking blood pressure, for instance. Others may be of little medical value but are ritually important — wearing masks in the delivery room, for instance. Many have both ritual and medical importance — episiotomy, for instance.

I have already suggested that birth is the key event in a series of changes and adjustments which make up our version of *couvade*: those rituals which occur in societies where there is some uncertainty about paternity. When it is clear to everyone who is father to the child, these rituals are less common or less important.

There is more to the ritual of birth than its role in couvade. It not only helps to give certainty to the question of *who* the father is, but also *what he is supposed to do*. When the father's role is clearly defined he will be less likely to need ritual to support and prepare him for it. But when there is uncertainty, we may expect rituals to become much more important. Having a baby is not just a matter of giving birth; it is also the time when the woman and man assume their new roles as mother and father.

Nearly every culture in the world marks this change with some ritual events. The details may vary, but the form is largely constant. They belong to a class of rituals known to anthropologists as *rites of passage*. These are found whenever a person changes his or her social status: initiation ceremonies mark the transition from child to adult; wedding ceremonies mark the transition from single to married; funeral ceremonies mark the transition from living to dead; and so on. Birth rituals mark the transition to parenthood — and in particular, as far as I am concerned here, the transition to fatherhood.

A rite of passage has three main parts — each of which may last for quite a long time, and consist of a number of different ritual activities. The rite of passage is only completed when all three parts have been performed.

In the first part — *the rite of separation* — the person undergoing the social change is separated from his old environment. This is often achieved by removal to a special place, set apart from normal life — a sacred initiation ground or building. Rites of cleansing and purifying often take place, and new clothing may be worn.

In Western birth practice there are many elements to parallel this. There is normally a journey to a place set apart — the hospital — where husband and wife will be separated from normal society and from each other. He is often left alone while his partner is taken off to be 'prepared'.

He suddenly becomes very aware of his lack of status and no-one seems to know or care what is supposed to happen to him. Several of the men interviewed by Joel Richman felt that their wives were being taken back into a 'society of women', and one said that it was as if he was being punished for imposing the burden of pregancy on his wife.

When the prospective father is allowed to meet his partner again she will have been 'admitted', and will now be firmly incorporated in the hospital routine. The fact that the father is not formally admitted is another sign of his more marginal status, but before he is allowed into the labour ward he will be obliged to put on some special clothing. Different hospitals have different degrees of strictness about this, but the full kit consists of overshoes, gown, hat and mask. This clothing has little or no practical value, but it has a clear symbolic function. It emphasizes that the father is unclean and needs to be transformed by being covered in pure (usually white) robes before being allowed into the inner sanctum of the labour room.

Clothing in hospital has another function: to mark the status of the various individuals involved in the drama. The higher the status the less important it is to wear protective clothing. If the chief obstetrician looks in to see how things are progressing he may well not bother to wear any special clothing at all. The houseman in charge of the labour will wear a gown, but may leave it untied. The nurses will wear neatly starched, tightly fitting uniforms, while the father, at the bottom of the heap, has to wear shapeless ill fitting garments which might almost have been designed just to make him look and feel stupid.

The middle stage of a rite of passage is called the *liminal* period (from the Latin for *threshold*), when those undergoing the rite have no status of any kind. They have left their old roles behind (they are often spoken of as having died — especially in initiation rites), but have not yet adopted their new roles. During this liminal period they may be subjected to humiliation and strict discipline. In some initiation ceremonies, pain may be inflicted on those being initiated, and the liminal period may be climaxed by some bodily mutilation (circumcision, knocking out of a tooth, scarification, etc). Most important of all, there is instruction — often in symbolic form — about the nature of society and what is expected of the new role for which the person is being prepared. The liminal stage may last from less than an hour in a wedding service, to over a month in some initiation ceremonies.

Again, the parallels are clear. The woman in labour has little status in the hospital. Her partner has even less. Both of them may feel humiliated by their treatment: by the way that her natural functions are taken over by strangers; by the way that he may be told to leave the room without any explanation; by the way their questions may not be answered to their satisfaction.

The liminal stage of birth lasts from the time the mother is admitted and labour becomes well established until several days after the birth. A common pattern is for the woman to remain in hospital throughout this period, although there has been a recent trend towards shorter stays — especially for second and subsequent deliveries. During her time in hospital the mother will suffer a lot of pain and discomfort. Her partner does not suffer in the same way of course, although he can often become very distressed by the experience of her suffering. But he also may have to put up with some minor physical discomfort; having to go for many hours without rest or food because there are no facilities for him in most hospitals.

There is a lot of teaching in this phase, but it is couched in symbolic terms and does not have the formal nature we normally associate with the word *teaching*. It is more an expression and reinforcement of certain key social ideas and attitudes which have a direct bearing on styles of parenthood. Again I concentrate on the messages which are being picked up by the father, although the effect on the mother is probably even greater.

Because both mother and father have little or no status a bond of common suffering is forged between them. This has been observed in many other rite of passage situations, especially in initiation rites. It can give the couple in birth a new closeness and a new respect for each other. Many men are able to appreciate and admire the female in a way that they might not have done before. Often there is a mixture of awe and regret:

> My wife was so good, she was terrific the way she handled it. She had depths of energy and power that I didn't realize she had, and I felt envious that I couldn't do it as well. (*John*).
>
> I really did feel envious of the fact of giving birth, because no matter how close you are to the child, I mean the fact that you didn't physically give birth to that child — I don't know, it's a physical involvement, whereas a man's involvement is emotional, intellectual, whatever. It's not physical. (*Stuart*)

This is another important message. A man is brought up to interact with the world in physical ways and to mistrust feelings. Now he discovers that fatherhood is different. It is *not* physical, but requires those very emotions which he tends to play down. Furthermore, he learns that fatherhood is not primary — it always follows motherhood and does not stand on the same secure physical base that motherhood does.

Most men want to be present at birth because they see it as their duty to help. But the father's job as a labour companion serves to reinforce the secondary nature of his role. A good labour companion must be subordinate to the woman in labour: *her* wishes and needs are paramount. In the same way, the message of the rite suggests, fatherhood is subordinate to motherhood.

Because this message conflicts with the desire for equality, many men are moving towards greater participation in birth. They try to do this in two ways. Firstly there is a move towards greater emotional involvement. The *experience* of childbirth is becoming ever more important to men, as we saw in chapter five. Lacking the physical basis of parenthood that mothers have, fathers are trying to establish a secure emotional base on which to build. To the extent that the ritual allows them to do this, it is expressing and enacting the ideals of active fatherhood. Indeed, for many men, this is the closest they will ever get to it.

The other way men try to express their involvement in the birth process is by *coaching*. The status of man as labour coach is a difficult one, full of ambiguities. On the one hand it can be an acceptance of the futility of trying to identify too closely with the labouring woman, on the other it can be an attempt to 'take over' and control the woman's reproductive function.

If coaching is used as an expression of complementarity it can strengthen the values of active fatherhood. The father recognizes that there are differences between mother and father, but does not accept that this means a lack of equality. Rather, the two can work together; each doing what they are best able to do in the current situation. One way in which this can be seen is in relations with the hospital staff.

If the medical staff want the couple to behave in a certain way, or to agree to some obstetric intervention, they often express themselves in terms of the health of the baby, instead of trying to relate to the couple directly. While there are clearly times when this is appropriate, there are others when intervention has no obvious medical reason. Many fathers feel that they have a special role to play at such times.

One of the doctors, I think he was — something to do with the birth anyway — came in and said, "The waters haven't burst yet, we're going to burst them for you." And we said, "What for, we're perfectly OK." And he said, "Well, do you want to put the baby at risk?" And it's a difficult thing to say, but you've got to say, "I don't think we want the waters burst, thank you." I suppose you've got to push them a bit. Because if it really is a risk they'll push you out of the way anyway. But the man's important here I think because he can stand up — the woman's often flat on her back. (*John*)

In fact, the doctor did go away and let the labour take its course naturally. This is a typical obstetric encounter, significant not only for its use of the baby's safety as a threat, but also in the lack of explanation or even introduction given by the doctor. It illustrates the distinctive role which the father in labour often feels called upon to play; namely that it is his responsibility to deal with the hospital's authority structures. So something which starts off by attempting to establish an equality based on complementary roles takes on the appearance of the ideology of traditional fatherhood, with its stress on the father's role as mediator with the outside world.

Power relations are expressed in other ways in the birth ritual. The hospital authorities are not only in a position of superior status to the couple having the baby — a common situation in rites of passage — but there are also very strict hierarchies operating amongst the staff themselves, which are symbolized by the differences in dress and behaviour. In this way the hierarchical basis of our society is displayed to the new parents as a model which they ought to emulate.

The father may be tempted to accept this model and try to carve out a niche for himself in the power structure by using his role as labour coach to gain status in the obstetric hierarchy and show dominance over his wife. In such a situation, where differences of power and status are clearly revealed, many men find it hard not to join in the power games. The extent to which he is encouraged or discouraged in these games is crucial to the exact message of the rite — something which is still in a state of flux.

Despite all the undercurrents of power and domination, by the time of the delivery itself the prevailing feelings are of involvement and equality between new mother and father. This is the high point of the rite, and the values celebrated now are those associated with active, rather than traditional, fatherhood.

In chapter five I suggested that a sexual metaphor could provide some insights into a man's experience of birth. The account I gave there (loosely based on the birth of our second child, Adam) ended with the all-too-soon intervention of the staff, unwilling or unable to halt the implacable

steamroller of hospital routine. If birth is like an orgasm, then the period after birth is like the *petit mort*; that small, glorious, moment when you are dead to the world of desire — and thus replete. It does not last forever, but that experience of fulfillment could remain as a powerful influence for years to come.

Unfortunately, for many new parents this beautiful moment is made ugly and unclean by the intrusion of medical science. It may be in the shape of the jovial obstetrician with his shining needle and thread, come to sew up the cut or tear which marked the new child's passage into the world, or it may simply be the bustling nurse anxious to get the mother into the hospital machine, and the father out of it. Either way, the father is suddenly a stranger at the nativity, no longer an actor but just an unwelcome part of the audience to be hustled out of the theatre now that the show is over.

The father is an embarrassment to the obstetric tailor as he merrily sews the mother's vagina and says that, thanks to *his* expertise, sex will now be better than ever. "She'll fit you like a glove, ha, ha." Of course he's embarrassed — who wouldn't be? That's why he wants the father out of the way. And the nursing staff are perhaps embarrassed too. The more powerful the emotions that the new parents are able to express — and many men cry for the first time in their adult lives when they are present at the birth of their first child — the more it may seem like a voyeuristic intrusion for the staff to have to be present.

It isn't always like this. In many hospitals a new understanding is arising, and now, when the circumstances have been right and everyone has worked together with mutual respect, all can rejoice together and there is no discomfort or sense of intrusion. But even here the moment is not allowed to last; cannot be allowed to last. For it would subvert the system. Normal power relations must be resumed as soon as possible — and that means returning the mother to her subordinate status as a 'patient' and expelling the father as irrelevant. So out he goes.

This isn't the end of the rite. The new father is still in that marginal state; still becoming a father, rather than truly being a father. The physical act of birth is not enough. He must also assume the social role of fatherhood, and this he cannot do — at least until mother and child join him. For the time being he is still in limbo. Like most of the men I have spoken to, I remember the alienation of that experience just as vividly as the joy of the birth itself.

It always seemed to be three o'clock in the morning when I left the hospital after the birth of one of my children. No matter what the rest of the world thought, the streets were always dark and empty, with only the sound of my footsteps disturbing the silence. Occasionally I might see other people, but always in the distance — with no possibility of interaction. I seemed to be disengaged, a zombie living in my own time stream; a dream time when nothing happens and everything is possible.

Like a creature of myth, you feel capable of anything. But, filled with the knowledge of your fertile life-creating power, you discover that in fact you are impotent. Despite this power you cannot touch the world in any way. And so you wander aimlessly through those night streets until you arrive at home, or at some other destination which ought to have meaning. But the real meaning is locked away in a bed in a ward in a building where you are not welcome. It isn't that reality is hard to come back to, rather that reality refuses to allow you in.

During this difficult part of the rite of passage there are a few simple ritual exercises to help the father to cope. One of the most important is letting other people know about the birth. This seemingly simple activity is in fact rich with social meaning. Whom do you tell first, and how? I guess that the current social expectation is that you should ring her parents first, closely followed by your own. But the order and speed with which you inform other relatives, friends and well-wishers will tell you much about the way you structure your social networks, and who you count most important.

It is in just such small ways as this that we constantly create and reaffirm our society and our culture. In this case the new father is making decisions about the nature of his own social universe and is starting to regain contact with the external world.

Getting back into the world is not a quick or simple process — especially while the new parents are kept apart by those institutions in society which like to refer to themselves as the 'caring professions'. The new father has a great desire for company. What he really wants, more than anything, is to be with his partner and child. Not just to talk and to look, but to touch; especially to touch. It is cuddling and consolation and mutual comforting that he desires. There is so much newness to explore together that there is an almost physical pain in the separation.

Several studies, including Masters and Johnson's famous work on human sexuality, have suggested that many men start an affair just after the birth of their child. On the face of it, this seems a particularly callous and cynical thing to do. While his wife is shut up in the hospital caring for their new baby, he is out behaving badly, caring only for his own pleasure. But I don't think it is quite as simple as that. The new father wants physical contact; he needs to express himself and his feelings through the medium of touch. He is denied access to the one person he really wants to be with. Even at visiting time he is expected to behave in a frigid and non-physical manner — as befits a place where people are sick and dying.

So he turns to another woman. Perhaps they've been close friends for a long time, perhaps they've never really been more than acquaintances or colleagues at work. But his vulnerability appeals to her — brings out her maternal instinct, if you like — and when he turns to her for physical support she is there to help him. Men often have the problem of being unable to distinguish the sensual from the sexual; of wanting to express all closeness in terms of making love. Given the increased awareness of their own sexuality which many men have after birth, it is hardly surprising that some find themselves tumbling into affairs almost by accident and almost against their wills.

The messages in this part of the rite have been powerful, but they do little to reinforce the active model of fatherhood which the earlier part promoted. On the contrary, the father is now learning that while motherhood is full-time (she stays in hospital with the baby), fatherhood is part-time (he visits her when he can, or when he is allowed to). He also discovers that fatherhood restricts intimacy between husband and wife. If he wants any physical comfort, whether sexual or not, he must get it from another woman or else go without.

It is hard to imagine a more curious way of treating new fathers than the one we presently operate. They are invited — pressured — to attend and participate in the birth of their children. Their emotional involvement is increasingly tolerated and encouraged, and then — just when the new parents need each other most — the father is forcibly separated from mother and child. If the father was not involved at all, his absence after the birth would not be bearable. But to start a process and then suspend it at its climax seems almost gratuitously cruel.

The way we handle the liminal part of our birth rite certainly is unusual. There are many patterns throughout the world, but I don't know of another culture which encourages the father to be present at birth and then expels him before the rite is finished. Many societies exclude men from the birth itself and also keep mother and father separated for a long period - thirty days or more is not uncommon. Some exclude men from birth, but allow them unrestricted access to the mother and child afterwards. Others expect the father to assist his wife in labour and then to aid her at home while she is sheltered from most household tasks for the first two weeks of the baby's life. An extension of this in some cultures requires both parents to be isolated for a period. Their meals are brought to them by relatives and they are left alone to get to know themselves again as a family.

If the logic of active fatherhood is followed through this latter course would seem to be the obvious one to adopt: include men at birth and then seclude them with the mother and child for a period afterwards. After all, there is now great concern that mothers should be allowed unrestricted access to their new babies so that they can *bond* properly. 'Bonding' has now become excessively fashionable, and has even achieved breakthrough into the popular consciousness. In fact there is an analogous word for fathers, coined as long ago as 1974 by Greenberg and Morris. They used the term *engrossment* to describe a kind of euphoric involvement between a father and his newly born child. Yet so far there has not been a movement to allow fathers unrestricted access to their new babies so that they can 'engross' properly![18]

Recently there have been some tentative moves in this direction. In the US, where childbirth is becoming ever more competitive, a number of hospitals now offer double rooms for the new father and mother. Some even advertise a champagne dinner for the couple to celebrate the birth! The main drawback is that it is simply too expensive for most people to be able to stay more than two or three nights.

In Britain things are less advanced. One hospital in East Anglia has started allowing fathers to stay with their wives after the birth — but only when the baby has to go into special care. This innovation has not been universally praised. At one local meeting of the Royal College of Midwives, many of the midwives present felt very threatened by the idea. They did not think that it was 'proper' for a man and woman to be sharing a bed in a hospital, where the sexes are usually rigidly separated. Perhaps they were also worried about having a part of the hospital which was private and where they would have needed to ask permission to enter. At another hospital, during a discussion about the equipment needed to set up a new maternity unit, the director of nursing said she would like at least one double bed in the unit. "Going to climb into bed with the patients, are you?" sneered one of the consultant obstetricians.

Although these attitudes may not be very enlightened, in a sense they are right. Hospital is *not* the best place for perfectly healthy people to stay in order to get to know each other as a family. Not only are they designed for sick people, they are also expensive places to run, with highly trained staff. It is a waste of resources to use them as hotels for new parents. Perhaps home birth could be the answer. It certainly has one obvious advantage: since he is on his own territory, no-one is able to throw the new father out onto the streets!

Yet even at home things don't always go as people hope. Jimmy and Sara's second child was born at home. The delivery turned out to be rather more complicated than anticipated because the baby was the wrong way round. Jimmy had expected it to be a better experience than in hospital, but in the end found it harder to cope with. The midwife also seemed to find it difficult — especially in dealing with Jimmy himself. She was quite a lot older than Sara and Jimmy, but he felt very matronized by her, particularly the way she kept calling him "young Jimmy". After the birth, the midwife took the baby away to bath it. Jimmy felt very excluded by this. "She should have let me do it", he said afterwards.

Despite this, most people who have experienced both home and hospital birth prefer the home birth. But at this point in obstetric history home birth is clearly a minority interest. Perhaps economic pressures will eventually bring hospital birth to an end, but it will take time.

The ideal, from the point of view of supporting the values of commitment and involvement, is a place where the new parents and baby could stay for a couple of weeks after the birth. Perhaps some kind of birth centre where they can spend time getting to know each other and being made a fuss of by family, friends and society as a whole. Despite the fact that birth itself has been institutionalized, becoming a parent remains a very private thing with little support from other people. Such a birth centre could help new parents to feel more valued, and help them to make a positive transition to their new roles. More involvement from society might also help to solve the problem of the ending of the rite of passsage for birth.

In a complete rite of passage the liminal period ends with a *rite of incorporation*. This moves the subject back into the world, but now in his or her new status: as adult; as husband or wife; as parent. This new status will be publicly announced and celebrated. There may be feasting and general rejoicing, and those who have undergone the ritual will be granted privileges because of their new status, and accorded a new respect by society at large.

The parallel with Western birth rites breaks down here. Although the first two stages are highly elaborated in Western obstetrics, there is little or no rite of incorporation. We leave the rite of passage unfinished; the new mother and father may be reunited, but they are left in limbo, having to fend for themselves as best they can. Because the obstetric hierarchy sees birth principally in terms of delivering a healthy baby it tends to ignore the wider emotional and social needs of the new parents.[19]

To many people the ritual of birth seems pointless — even gratuitously cruel. Feminist writers identify obstetric ritual with male dominance and a desire to control female fertility. There is a lot of truth in this view, yet there is also evidence to suggest that the humiliation and control has a purpose, and that ultimately the rite could be beneficial and life-enhancing.

William Sargant is a psychologist who has written about the mechanism of initiation rites. He suggests that the intensity of the rite is like brainwashing or ecstatic religious conversion, and that it acts to make the subject more amenable to suggestion and able to make radical changes in outlook and belief. In this state of heightened suggestibility, the person being initiated can be more quickly and effectively conditioned to his new, adult, place in society. It is possible that all rites of passage are able to have similar effects. They may have unpleasant aspects, but their end result is beneficial, enabling a major change in lifestyle to be accepted quickly and easily.

The same should apply to Western birth ritual. It separates a man and woman from their normal environment, and subjects them to humiliation and disorientation in a strange setting where they are powerless and emotionally involved. At the end of this they should be welcomed back into society, honoured as a parents, and nurtured and supported in their new status. In this way the obstetric procedures necessary to bring about successful childbirth, and the ritual procedures necessary to bring about a successful transition to parenthood should run in parallel. In theory, this mix of science and ritual will produce physically healthy babies and socially well-adjusted parents. In practice, it doesn't seem to work so well.

Rites of passage appear in almost every known culture. The content and the symbols involved may change, but the form is constant. It is unlikely that such a rite would be so widespread if it did not fulfill a basic human social need. Regardless of any psychological mechanisms, the rite has its own logic and structure. If the pattern is disrupted or left incomplete, serious distress could result. In order for any heightened suggestibility to have positive consequences, there must be a nurturing and welcoming climax to the rite of passage. Otherwise the participant is left high and dry; alienated and distressed.

Some writers have suggested that there is a link between 'high technology birth' and postnatal depression in women. Others stress the high levels of circulating oestrogen in the newly delivered mother and see these as influential. I think that the incompleteness of the ritual and the contradictory messages it gives to parents may also have a part to play.[20]

I am often asked if men suffer from postnatal depression. This is a hard question to answer because the term itself is not precise, and because it tends to be defined exclusively in terms of women's experiences. It is possible to distinguish three different kinds of bad reaction after birth: all of which have been included under the umbrella of 'postnatal depression'.

Firstly, there is *postnatal psychosis*, a complete or partial mental breakdown precipitated by the birth, which often requires hospitalization. Both men and women can suffer from this illness. Symptoms for men include suicidal wishes, excessive drinking, irresponsible and lavish spending, or worries that an incurable disease has been contracted. Male postnatal psychosis is rare, but has been well documented.

The most common form of depression after childbirth is often known by women as *baby blues*. The symptoms are feelings of inadequacy, disorientation, despair and general lethargy. Fortunately, baby blues doesn't last very long; often no more than a couple of days. Many men have similar feelings of rejection, emptiness and dissociation after birth. I suggested earlier that these are a symptom of the separation experienced by new fathers when they leave hospital alone. Certainly, they often seem to disappear when the family is re-united at home. Another explanation was suggested to me by a father. "It's withdrawal symptoms after the 'high' of the birth", he said.

There are many people who believe that baby blues is linked to high postnatal hormone levels in the mother. If so, men's and women's reactions must have a different cause, since men are not, as far as I know, subject to high levels of female sex hormones after childbirth. On the other hand, if men's depression is a result of the birth experience, perhaps this is a significant factor in baby blues as well.

The term postnatal depression itself is usually reserved for a longer-term reaction. The symptoms are similar to those experienced in baby blues, but they persist — sometimes for months — and can be emotionally crippling to the new mother who has to try to cope with them. Brian Jackson claimed that a third of the men in his sample had clear symptoms of depression. But he didn't say enough to allow us to be able to tell how long this depression lasted, or how serious it was. Charlie Lewis (1986, p.84) cites two unpublished studies which also suggest that about one third of new fathers suffer from depression in the first few weeks after the birth. Nevertheless, the existing evidence clearly suggests that women have worse reactions than men, but it is impossible to be clear about this until more research has been done.

Whether or not some forms of postnatal depression are related to the structure and content of our birth rituals, it is clear that we have a problem with the way we handle birth at the moment. Because there is no proper conclusion to our rite for birth, society is sending out some very ambiguous messages about the status and role of fatherhood. But it should cause us no surprise to discover that these messages accurately reflect the contradictions experienced by the modern father as he attempts to reconcile the ideology of involved fatherhood with the constraints imposed by the outside world.

8. Feeding and Loving

The early days after the birth often confound expectations. Many men find it hard to relate to a new baby, often not really being involved until she is sitting up, or even walking and talking. Many women find similar difficulty, and society makes it even harder for them with its insistence on the 'maternal instinct' which any proper mother is supposed to have. The existence of such an instinct (or any corresponding 'paternal instinct') is very hard to demonstrate, but it still gives many new parents unrealistic expectations of their response to the new baby.

Sometimes the surprise is of the opposite kind — as David discovered. He was an insurance salesman in his early forties when he had his second child, a daughter. His first daughter had been born twenty years earlier, during his first marriage. He described himself as being a typical traditional father then — he'd been out drinking with his mates while she was being born, and had been almost completely uninvolved with her until she was nearly grown up. This time things were different. He had been enthusiastically present at the birth, and was determined to get involved and make up for all he had missed first time around.

He came along to several meetings of our fathers' group and was always a vocal contributor. One evening he turned to me and said, "You won't approve of this but every time I lie with my daughter on my chest, skin to skin, I get these really sexual feelings". Clearly, the spectre of incest had raised itself in his mind. Fortunately, I was spared the necessity of having to say anything because another father, rather more self-assured than David, immediately said, "Yeah, I know just what you mean. It happens to me too". A couple of the other men nodded as well, and the tension passed.

As we discussed it further it became clear that many men are quite unprepared for just how physical a new baby can be. It's easy to be wise after the event, because it is rather obvious when you think about it: all a baby does is to eat, sleep and excrete — all very physical things. If you want to communicate with a baby you must do it in a physical way; there is no other. Because many men have difficulty distinguishing the sensual from the sexual (not that there is any hard dividing line) some will always tend to interpret their own physical response to the baby in sexual terms.[21]

David's case illustrates yet another of the fundamental changes which seem to have occurred in the last thirty years or so. The more traditional models of fatherhood imply that even a committed father has relatively little involvement with babies - he doesn't take much interest until they are at least old enough to talk. Today, with the shift towards a more active style of fatherhood, men are expected to be involved right from the start. As ever, the reasons for this are complex, and often lead to conflict and anxiety in the new family.

New fathers enjoy the chance to show off their skills with the baby, but they don't often get the chance. One consequence of the separation of the new father from his wife and child after birth is that he often feels incompetent in the early weeks. Not only has she had longer to get to know the baby, but the very fact of his exclusion carries the message that he is relatively less important. Furthermore, he often *is* less competent than she, because no-one ever bothered to teach him such 'unmanly' skills as dressing or changing a baby.

Charlie Lewis found that many of the men in his sample had little or no involvement in child care. This was partly because they did not feel competent, partly because they couldn't be bothered, and partly because they were excluded by their wives. Of all the child care tasks, bathing was the one least often performed by these men. The following dialogue may help to reveal some of the hidden tensions behind the bare facts:

> *Interviewer*: Have you ever bathed him?
> *Father*: Yes.
> *Wife*: Not alone, you haven't.
> *Father*: I've splashed him.
> *Wife*: I'm holding him ... don't I? You only splash him.
> *Interviewer* (to husband): Is there any reason why you haven't bathed him yourself?
> *Wife*: I'd sooner trust myself. ... It's not that I don't trust him. I'd sooner do it myself where water comes in.

> *Interviewer* (to husband): So you would rather trust Sandra [wife] than yourself?
> *Father*: No...I'd do it.
> (Quoted in *Lewis*, 1986, p.100)

Actually, in my experience, men often do bath babies. Indeed, it is something which a man can often do better than his wife, because his hands will probably be bigger than hers and better able to support the baby. As the child gets bigger, he will be able to go in the big bath with dad and this is much appreciated.

> One of the things I enjoy is having the baby in the bath with me; we don't use the baby's bath any more. The wife usually brings me a cup of tea when I'm in the bath, so she brings the baby up as well and just plonks it in the bath with me, and that's really good. The only thing I dislike about it is he usually pees over me. (*Ian*)

> The really funny thing is when they start to talk, and they — I mean Elizabeth was sitting in the bath with me and she looked down and went "big tummy" — accurate, but cruel. (*Stuart*)

Even nappy changing is now acceptable to many men. It used to be the symbol of men's lack of involvement in child care that they would never change a dirty nappy. Fewer and fewer men still feel this way. Indeed, at one fathers' meeting I actually heard a man extolling the virtues of nappy changing, suggesting that it was a rather mystical time of communion between parent and child. No-one else present was entirely convinced, but some did agree that are times when changing a baby can be fun — provided there's no smelly mess to clear up. Babies often seem to be especially alert and attentive when lying on a changing mat waiting for clean clothes.

Nevertheless, matters such as bathing and changing often seem peripheral to many men. Feminist writers sometimes claim that men are not *really* involved in child care because they do fewer of the dirty, routine and tedious tasks such as bathing, washing, changing etc. Interestingly, more and more men agree that they are not really involved in child care — but precisely because all they do is bathing, washing, changing etc. These tasks are seen by some men as peripheral to the core child care activities, such as cuddling, tending, and — most especially — feeding.

Even those men and women who say that there is no real difference between fathers and mothers frequently mention breastfeeding as the one

Unconstructive Suggestions — the helpless father being matronised.

exception. Some men express real regret that they are unable to breastfeed.

> I really wanted Joan to breastfeed, it's the best thing isn't it, but I felt really frustrated and angry that I couldn't do it too. I was really jealous of her, it was an area of care that I was completely excluded from. (*Jim*)

Jim and Joan decided before their baby, Simon, was born that they would each work part time in order to be able to share the child care. They also decided that they would keep Simon in constant contact with one or other of them until he was able to walk. From then until he was two years old one of them would always be in sight, although if Simon chose to leave the room they would happily let him go off by himself. The intention was to promote a strong sense of security and also independence in Simon. He is now five and, according to Jim, is the most self-possessed and independent child in his class at school.

Jim's commitment to parenting is unusual, and perhaps extreme, and so was his reaction to breastfeeding. But his attitude to feeding was extreme only in the strength with which it was expressed. Most of the other men in the group agreed with him that breastfeeding was a real problem for any man who wants to be involved as a father. Another expression of this longing can be seen in a story which is widely told whenever parents start talking about men and breastfeeding. It is said that a man of forty, living in New York, was so keen to breastfeed his baby daughter that he paid for a course of injections of 'female sex hormone' which enabled him to develop breasts and produce milk. He was able to feed his daughter for about three months and she apparently coped well with the experience.

There are various versions of this story current, and one of them may reflect a true event, although I have been unable to find any definitive evidence that men can lactate.[22] The important thing is that the idea of men breastfeeding is now being openly discussed, and even though the vast majority of men and women reject it, they do so with that slightly fascinated interest with which many of them would also approach *Playboy* or *Mayfair*. It may not be right, but there is a certain attraction which is hard to dismiss.

So why do women discuss male lactation with embarrassed giggles? Why do men discuss female lactation with resentment and a sense of loss?

Why does breastfeeding provoke such powerful responses? Part of the answer lies, once again, in the uncertainty of paternity. Fatherhood can no longer be assumed as a biological given, but is a relationship which must be continually created by the father. One of the best ways of forging a kinship link of this kind is for the individuals involved to have some substance in common, for there to be something for them to share. The most obvious example of this is the sharing of 'blood'. We no longer believe that parents literally transmit blood to their offspring, but the idiom is still very much alive. We say that parent and child are 'blood relations', that they are the 'same flesh and blood', that 'blood will out', and so on.

Although blood is the most potent symbol of shared substance, it is not the only one. Shared food can also serve to build a relationship. This can be seen most clearly among some of the peoples of New Guinea and the South Pacific. Like us, they use kinship terms in two ways: both to denote 'true' kinsmen and also by extension to other people whose relationship is similar to a kinship relationship. Thus we may require our young children to call an adult friend of the family *uncle* or *aunt* even though there is no blood relationship. Similarly, a union leader may address the workers as *brothers*, or a feminist address her fellow women as *sisters*. There is no confusion in our minds about who is 'really' related to us, and the same is true throughout the world.

What is unusual about parts of New Guinea is that, although the people normally trace kinship through ties of blood just as we do, and use kinship terms for both true and honorary kinsmen, they will also say that some children who are *not* related by blood are true kinsmen. The reason for this seems to be that such a child has shared his father's food and this is sufficient to make a relationship of *true* kinship. Among the Arapesh of New Guinea this idea is so strong that Arapesh fathers, who are heavily commited to their children and very involved in childcare, do not base their paternal authority by reference to any ties of blood, but rather to shared food. It is this which makes the relationship between father and child.

If sharing food can create true kinship, this is especially true of sharing food with a new-born baby. Women who adopt young babies frequently want to breastfeed them. Although this is not easy, especially if the adoptive mother has never been pregnant herself, it can be done. But it requires a dedication and constant effort which is hard to explain except in terms of the woman wanting to make the baby hers by feeding it with her own life-giving milk. No man — except the fabulous New Yorker — can go this far, but it helps to explain a lot of men's feelings about breastfeeding. Bottle feeding seems to be more democratic. Since both parents can feed with the bottle the father is not put at a disadvantage.

It is a painful irony that the very men who are most tempted to bottle feed, because they are commited as fathers, are also the very men most likely to be convinced of the advantages of breastfeeding. They simply can't win — although more and more are attempting a compromise. This involves the mother expressing her breast milk so that the father can feed the baby himself, but without having to resort to infant formula with all its attendant disadvantages. The bottle manufacturers have now seized on this as a way of selling more products, since sales have been hit by the increase in breastfeeding. Several companies now use slogans such as, *A breastfed baby doesn't have to be fed by mum; Even dad can do it!*; or *Breastfeeding? Two can play at that game!* The infant formula companies have been using the same approach for several years now, informing us that one of the 'advantages' of bottle feeding is that men can do it too. Feeding with expressed breast milk may seem like an ideal solution to some, and it can obviously work on an occasional basis — it gives the breastfeeding mother a break, apart from anything else. But I doubt whether it's really a good solution for long-term or regular use.

The sucking action needed to get milk from a bottle is different from the suckling action needed to persuade a breast to give out milk. Some babies manage to switch from one to the other without any problem, but others become so confused that they can't do both. Since it is easier to get milk from a bottle than from the breast, most babies take the line of least resistance and start to reject the breast. This in turn means that the mother's milk supply will decline, there will be no milk for her to express, and so the baby will end up on formula anyway.

In the end, the man who feels jealous of his wife's ability to breastfeed has to accept that his reaction, although perfectly natural, is incapable of being cured. If other people were more sympathetic about his disappointment it might be easier to accept it as just one more of the inevitable adjustments and compromises which have to be made by both parents after the birth of a baby.

Other men are in favour of bottle feeding for much the same reason as they are fascinated by the machines and fetal monitors during childbirth: it is more 'scientific'. Indeed, this is the way that the idea of artificial feeding was originally marketed. Each 'authority' would have his (they were invariably male) own scientifically worked out 'formula' for a wonderful breast milk substitute. A 1902 advertisement for Allenburys' Foods describes itself as "A progressive dietary adapted to the physiological development of the child". It quotes a medical journal's opinion of it:

The system is well conceived, and if carried out exactly and scientifically should certainly and can, as we are able to personally testify, give most excellent results. The objects which are fulfilled by the method are manifold.

The style may have changed, but the message has not. Some people still feel that bottle feeding is more scientific — after all, they say, you can see exactly how much the baby is taking (although, since you can't see into a baby's stomach to see how full it is, this seems to be a dubious 'advantage'). This is especially true of those men who feel incapable of letting things happen, but rather want always to impose their will on the world and mould it. Culture is 'better' than nature just because it is man-made. Animals eat raw food; civilized human beings display their superiority to the animals by eating cooked food.

For some people it is the same with infant feeding: animals suckle their young; should we not prove our superiority by refusing to do this and using a 'cultural' food instead? The argument falls down of course, because infant formula is just modified animal's milk. But this fact is discreetly ignored by the companies and their success can be measured by the fact that only a couple of years ago an English hospital nurse was heard to say, "No, we don't feed the babies on cow's milk, we give them formula". The fact is that the scientific evidence demonstrates conclusively that breast milk is superior to any substitutes and that, at their best, such substitutes can be no more than adequate.

Although it may have no scientific advantages, bottle feeding does have one psychological advantage over breastfeeding: a woman may find bottle feeding easier than breastfeeding if she has no support and encouragement. This is because the reflexes involved in breastfeeding, especially the 'let-down' or 'milk ejection' reflex, are very susceptible to the woman's emotional state. The breastfeeding mother often needs support and help in order to feed successfully. Studies have shown that perhaps the most important source of support for the breastfeeding woman today is her husband. Zarina Kurtz found that three-quarters of the women she interviewed said that their husbands had given them more help than anyone after leaving hospital. Men are increasingly aware of this responsibility and are prepared to accept it — even though it can cause them more problems. After all, if the mother mothers the baby, and the father mothers the mother, who mothers the father?

The stress of those early days can be very hard to cope with. A new baby is so real, so substantial, so intrusive. Up till then it had all been theory. You thought you knew what it was going to be like, but suddenly you discover that this had just been a fantasy. No-one ever mentioned any of the important things: such as how noisy a new baby is, or how frustrated, tense, and angry you can get when he won't stop crying. They never said what it would be like to go without proper sleep for days and nights on end; that you wouldn't be able to think straight or have any time for yourselves. They never explained that it can go on and on until there seems no chance of remission for good behaviour. And finally, no-one ever pointed out how alone you'd be: how after all the support and encouragement you got during pregnancy, you would now have to work it all out for yourselves.

Given all this — and more — it is not surprising that a new father can find himself torn between his desire to nurture and protect his wife and baby, and his own desire to be looked after. Even the most selfless man can find himself becoming jealous; jealous of his partner because she is no longer able to give him the time and attention she used to, and jealous of the baby because it has supplanted him as the centre of her affections. For many men this sense of isolation and rejection is made worse if she is breastfeeding, and it can take on a specifically sexual dimension.

Breasts are sex objects in our society. Most men in the West find them sexually stimulating both to sight and touch. They are still tabooed from general view, and their constant exposure in advertising, magazines and films only serves to reinforce this taboo. They play an important role in close relationships, and touching the breasts is an important expression of intimacy. Some men see breasts as 'theirs', almost as property. "I married her because of her breasts, they're mine, and I'm not going to have any kid touching them, including my own!" said an expectant father to Robert Bradley (p.173). Most men don't react so explicitly, but the feeling is there, and is often made manifest when breastfeeding starts.

I don't think that I am the most chauvinist of men (but then, whoever does?), but I found myself forced to confront my own feelings of ownership after the birth of Mark, our eldest. There was never any doubt in my mind about breastfeeding. I had been breastfed myself; Shirley was keen, and the hospital strongly advised it (there was a history of allergy on her side of the family). But I had a problem when she started feeding in front of other people. I found myself embarrassed and resentful. I didn't want 'my' breasts to be shown off — especially to other men. I don't think I mentioned this to anyone at the time, and I certainly didn't want Shirley to give up breastfeeding, so I just sat and inwardly writhed.

Gradually I got used to it, better able to separate the natural and sexual functions of the breasts. By the time Adam was born my prejudices had learned their lesson; never again did I suffer from feelings of possessive jealousy about breastfeeding. I have since spoken to other men about this. Some felt the same way, others never suffered from the problem at all. In a way it is trivial, but it illustrates just one of the unexpected traps for the unwary father.

Jealousy manifests itself in other ways as well: it's a key emotion. It is well known — almost a cliché — that men can 'feel left out of it' after a baby is born. For many men the breasts are an important part of lovemaking. But the fact is that the breasts are often — usually — tabooed after childbirth for one reason or another: she doesn't want them touched; they leak if they're touched; he feels they've become the baby's exclusive property. This means that for some months after the birth, at least until the milk supply is not so plentiful, and perhaps until weaning, an important part of lovemaking is prohibited. Now this is not the cause of that 'being left out' feeling, but it can be a contributory factor. More to the point, it appears to be something that can be cured. If the baby is put on the bottle, then I can have my breasts back, can't I?

These worries about breasts and breastfeeding are part of a larger set of problems relating to sex after childbirth. A woman who wrote to me on the subject said this:

> After the birth of my baby I felt quite ill for a considerable time and it took me a long time to adjust to the culture shock of becoming a mother, despite (or perhaps because of) having been a successful 'career' person. I felt I had no time to be a lover, was hard put to be a wife and seemed only to be able to manage to get the meals cooked — and that not always. When my husband and I finally managed to make love after the birth of our child it was not our first attempt. I was like a hesitant virgin for several months and could face so far and no more. Things improved, but I have always been somewhat dogged by night wakings, the residual feeling of being assaulted, etc. etc.

There are many reasons why sex after childbirth can be difficult. The trauma of the birth itself is often a major factor. Labour can be exhausting and it can take many weeks for a woman's body to recover fully. More important is that birth often leaves scars — even if it is a straightforward 'normal' birth. An episiotomy or a tear in the perineum can take a long time to heal and can be excrutiatingly painful at first. The altered hormonal balance after birth also makes it difficult for many women to get interested in sex, or to achieve orgasm easily, even if they do manage to make love.

These are the areas on which the baby books concentrate. The implication is always that they are transitory problems which will pass in a relatively short time, and that if they don't, then something 'abnormal' has occured. But psychological scars are often deeper than physical ones, and the feeling of violation experienced by many women can take much longer to get over. The woman whose body was taken over and controlled by obstetricians may fear sex as yet another assault and violation which she is simply unable to cope with — especially with the stress of adjusting to a new role with a new baby.

These reasons, plus many others such as tiredness, lack of opportunity, a woman's bad feelings about the changes in her body after birth, worries about contraception, and depression after childbirth mean that slow sexual adjustment is commonplace rather than rare. Yet the baby books continue to betray us by peddling a set of false assumptions:

> Lovemaking? She can't be bothered with it now, psychologically or physically. Wait — for about four weeks. (*Bradley*, p.163)

> There is a lot to be said for waiting until after your wife's postnatal examination at six weeks before making love again, not because there is anything magical about the six week period, but just because having been examined by her doctor and reassured by him that everything has returned to normal will make her much more confident about the whole idea. (*Fenwick*, p.161)

> It is not a good idea to put it off for too long, especially if there have been stitches for a tear or an episiotomy — the healing scar tissue can shrink too much so that the vagina narrows excessively. For most couples the time is between three and eight weeks after delivery. (*Brant*, p.156)

> It used to be said that a couple should wait several months before making love again. But this can be regarded as nothing but an old wives' tale — unless, of course there are definite contraindications. (*Trimmer*, p.65).

These quotes, all taken from books written by men and addressed to fathers, suggest a situation far removed from the reality of many new parents' experiences. The fact seems to be that many, perhaps most, women find their whole attitude towards sexuality and the physical aspects of lovemaking radically changed after childbirth, and *this change lasts for many months or years.* In quite a few cases the change is permanent. One antenatal teacher I know suggested that only one couple in twenty did *not* experience a severe disruption of their sex life. Indeed, given the major changes which a baby brings, this need not surprise anyone. The reason it causes so much distress is that, on the whole, it is only the woman whose attitude towards sexuality is changed. Her partner, who has not gone through the same *physical* experiences as she, is usually only too keen for a resumption of normal service.

We have seen that many men shy away from sexual activity during pregnancy. Although some authorities see this as a 'problem' to be solved, I have argued that it is a natural and normal male reaction to pregnancy, which should be accepted as such. There does not seem to be an equivalent common postnatal male shyness. Some men do not want sex after the baby has been born, but the majority do — and they want it very much. Again, the reasons are complex: besides his obvious physical desire, a new father needs cuddling and consolation. Men are sensitive to 'rejection' at the best of times; when a new baby has just elbowed them out the limelight it is even worse.

Yet despite the fact that most couples experience a more serious dislocation of their sex life than they were prepared for, we still try to pretend that things are not as they really are. Sara was talking to me about this recently. She still doesn't feel like making love — six months after the birth of their second baby. She puts it down to breastfeeding.[23] Her own lack of interest distresses her, although mainly for her husband's sake. I said that I thought that her reaction was much more common than usually recognized, and she gained some comfort from this. She said that she hoped that Jimmy would come along to the fathers' group so that he could discuss it with other men and come to realize that her lack of interest was natural. "Then he won't think I'm rejecting him", she said. But I had to point out that, even if he did understand, it wouldn't alter the fact that she was rejecting him. That is the fact which many couples have to face. At the moment many of them do so in a context of unrealistic expectations. But even if the situation is better understood, it is not automatically easier to cope with. We can understand and still resent. Comprehension does not neccessarily bring acceptance or approval.

However, in this case it may be that the expectations are helping to create the problem. Many societies taboo intercourse while a woman is still breastfeeding, often claiming that it will harm the child. Since weaning does not occur until the second year or later in most traditional societies, this often means a two-year period of abstinence for the new parents. Men in such circumstances seem to cope in different ways. Some, having more than one wife, may simply find legitimate sexual outlets elsewhere. In other cases adultery is the solution — but everything is very discreetly surrounded by a conspiracy of silence. In this way the man's physical needs may be satisfied without threat to his marriage. Sometimes the taboo is simply ignored, either because the husband insists, or by mutal agreement between husband and wife.

When a long period of abstinence is prescribed there is usually some kind of outlet for the husband's sexuality. But not always. The Grand Valley Dani of Papua New Guinea have become rather famous because of their apparent lack of interest in sex. According to Karl Heider, Dani parents *always* abstain from all sexual relations for four to six years after the birth of a child. Most of them have no alternate sexual outlets and none shows signs of unhappiness or frustration at this position.

We tend to assume that sexual activity is necessary and inevitable. There is often an undisguised scepticism about monks, priests or others who adopt a life of celibacy. Surely, we say, there must be something wrong with them, or else they must 'have a bit on the side'. Yet the evidence from them, from the Dani, from the behaviour of many men during pregnancy, shows that it is not necessarily so. People can live without sex, and there may be times in every person's life cycle when this is normal for them. If so, we do no-one a service by pressuring them into unrealistic expectations.

There are no easy answers to the problems of adjustment to parenthood. Lack of physical lovemaking is only one of them, although often the most obvious and painful. I think that it is important to recognize just how common, and perhaps inevitable, it is. This will not take away the pain of rejection, but it may help to ease it. No-one is to blame; not father, not mother, not baby. Having a baby is a greater change than most of us realize. It is not a temporary break in a relationship which will sooner or later will get back to the way things used to be. There is no going back after a baby. Even though there is some continuity, it is like a new beginning; almost as if you were meeting for the first time.

Because we pay a lot of attention to birth in our society, with many rituals of preparation and purification, there is a tendency to see it as an end in itself. But it is not; it is a beginning. And whether for good or ill, those first weeks and months of life after birth are the start of a new way of living.

9. The Father at Work

The making of the modern father is complete. The complex biological, ritual and social processes which create fatherhood have been performed. From now on it is a matter of living with the new role.

Unfortunately, for many men today, fatherhood is far from being a stable occupation. Earlier I suggested that styles of fathering could be arranged on a spectrum from *traditional* to *active*. These are characterized by two main qualities: the amount of participation in childcare, and the way power is exercised within the home. I also suggested that most men move towards the active end of the fatherhood spectrum during pregnancy and birth. But the new father can find himself under severe pressures which may push him back towards a traditional way of fathering. In this chapter I look at the way his desire for involvement in the home can be compromised, and in the next I will look briefly at domestic politics.

After the heady experience of birth and early days there is a gradual return to 'normality'. For most men the spectre of work now looms large. All that has happened during the year-long preparation for paternity is to be challenged by the work ethic and the conflict of interests and loyalties which it brings. Work and fatherhood often seem to be naturally incompatible; each demanding the father's principal loyalty. In such a situation different responses are possible. In particular, the relative importance given to home and work will vary from father to father.

The active father may start with quite a high work involvement, but when the pregnancy is confirmed he rapidly gives priority to home, and correspondingly decreases his commitment to work. By the time of the birth he is clear that his main attachment is to home and family. Some

active fathers, though by no means all, are involved in full-time care of their children. The common description of this — *role-swapping* — illustrates the problems they can have. The undisguised sexism of this term shows how strongly attached we still are to conventional stereotypes of men and women.

> After I tell [people] that I do the kids, they say, "Well, don't you do anything else?" It's almost impossible to make men understand. If you tell a woman, she understands, but to a man it just means you stay home all day. When I say I'm a lawyer, that seems to put me up a notch. I have to have a separate validity. It wouldn't matter if I was the worst lawyer in the world and the best father. (*Levine*, p.124)

The active father is always open to the reproach that he has unsexed himself; become effeminate. And in his darker moments he too may wonder about his masculinity. Because so much of our definition of maleness is tied up in the world of work, the active father's relative lack of commitment to it is a potential problem for his self-image.

At the opposite end of the spectrum is the traditional father. His fatherhood career is rather different. Although he, too, moves towards greater home involvement during pregnancy, he quickly veers back to high work involvement after the birth. It is important to remember that, within his definitions of fatherhood, this is not a denial of his paternal duty. Providing for the family is his key parental responsibility.

Dave is a real estate agent. At an antenatal class we talked about the impact of babies on work. He was very clear about his priorities. "My job comes first", he said. "A dozen other people depend on me for their livelihood and if I can't do my job properly they'll be out of work. I need my sleep as well. If the baby wakes a lot, then I'll just have to sleep on a couch in the office." Although no-one criticized Dave, there was a faint feeling of disapproval from the other couples in the room. Dave's wife said little; she was clearly prepared to accept the situation, but I got the feeling that she would rather that he wasn't quite so definite about things.

I spoke to Dave again when his daughter was about six months old. "We've been very lucky", he said. "She's only woken up once or twice during the night since she was four weeks old, so there's been no real problem with sleeping." Dave felt that he'd come over a bit stronger than he meant to at the antenatal class. The point he wanted to get over was his responsibility to his employees — in a sense they are his family too and so his options are not as simple as many men's. But the birth of Gemma has made a difference to his attitudes to work. He is more keen to get home now. "Before, if there was something which needed to be done, but wasn't absolutely urgent, I'd probably stay on and get it done. Now I'll leave it and get home earlier." Dave is also very aware of the extra responsibility which he has towards his wife and daughter. He is very committed to his home life, perhaps more so than he anticipated before the birth. In view of this, I asked him whether I was correct in putting him in the 'traditional' category. "I've never analyzed it, but I suppose I have to be by the nature of my job. If I had to work until 10 o'clock tomorrow night, then I would."

Dave's case not only illustrates the traditional, high work/low home, approach to fatherhood, but shows the complexity of fathering today. Dave is committed to fatherhood. If he had a different job, if he hadn't built up a successful business with responsibilities to both employees and customers, then he might have adopted a more active model of fatherhood.

Whatever their problems, those men who are committed to either traditional or active fatherhood do at least have a clear set of priorities with respect to home and work involvement. But in my experience an increasing number of modern fathers, who do not fall neatly into either category, try to give priority to *both* work and home. They don't want to lose the sense of freshness and fulfilment they can sense in fatherhood, nor do they want to lose the consolations of the familiar world of work. So they try to keep a foot in both camps. Not surprisingly they have a hard time, and may be doomed to failure in one or both fields. Can any man serve two masters?

One of the most serious conflicts between home and work revolves around the question of responsibility. Dave decided that his prime responsibility had to lie towards his staff and customers. After all, if you were selling your house and the agent decided that he couldn't get round to advertising it because his new baby had bad colic, you might be sympathetic but you wouldn't be very pleased. A colleague of mine had just such an experience recently while she was trying to move house. In her case, it was her lawyer who had just had a baby. In the middle of the transaction he decided that he needed to take two weeks paternity leave. Everything had to stop. Even after that, because he worked from home, he was often unavailable as he wanted to spend time with his new baby. It was easy to sympathize with his paternal desires, but it was hard on Mary who simply wanted to move house and became the innocent victim of his newborn child.

The conflict of interests in this case is obvious, and almost impossible to reconcile. Many workers are not faced with such a direct choice between family and 'customers'. Often the dilemma is between loyalty to home and a corporate loyalty of the sort which expects first call on a man's time and energy:

> "Ah, Tim. We'll have to work on for a few hours tonight I'm afraid. Head office have just decided that they want the Stanton report on Thursday, rather than next Monday. No problem, I take it?"

> "Well, actually Mr Dykes, I was rather hoping to get away a bit early today. It's my daughter's second birthday and she's having her first proper party. I said I'd be there."

> "Surely they can manage without you? Unless your wife is ill?"

> "No sir, she's fine. I just wanted to be there to share it with my daughter. I promised her."

> "Well Jones, all overtime is of course voluntary. You must make up your own mind about this. When you've done so, come and let me know whether a six figure account or a child's birthday party is more deserving of your attention. I await your decision with interest."

What would you do? We are increasingly subject to pressures to be more 'efficient'. Corporate loyalty is preached as a virtue and Japanese-style work methods are seen as the salvation of Western industry. With high unemployment there is ever-greater pressure to conform and knuckle under to pressure from above. Seldom can it have been harder for the working man who wants to make a commitment to his home. One of the problems faced by many new fathers is a lack of understanding and support from their employers and workmates — especially from the other fathers. The very people who might be expected to be most sympathetic are often the most hostile. Why should this be?

A similarly paradoxical result was discovered by Zarina Kurtz in her survey on breastfeeding support. She found that doctors (mainly male) were more supportive of breastfeeding women than nurses (mainly female). Furthermore, nurses who had children were less supportive than those without children. She suggested that this might be due to feelings of jealousy and resentment. Perhaps their own feeding had not gone as well as they would have liked, and their frustration got in the way of their support. I suspect that a similar sort of mechanism might also be operating in the office or factory. The successful manager is likely to have decided in favour of work rather than home. He has achieved his ambition, but the cost may have turned out to be higher than he thought. Because of his commitments to work he may find himself in his middle years almost a stranger to his children, wishing that he had spent more time and energy on them when they were younger.

Some of these men, the wisest, may use their experience to allow them to help their younger colleagues through the difficult work/home divide. But others will be jealous of the younger man. His commitment to home and family will seem like a criticism of the choices they had made. And for this reason the committed father will be resented rather than helped.

There is another problem experienced by many working fathers. Work requires a particular set of attitudes which are often inappropriate for childcare. To be successful at work you must be decisive, have clear goals, be able to make and accept deadlines, and perform specific tasks in a specified time. Young children don't work that way. For the first two or three years a young child does not have goals in an adult sense. She does things because they are good to do, not because they are steps towards an end. If something is worth doing once, it's probably worth doing a dozen or more times. A child can have endless patience at times, building up bricks and knocking them down over and over again. At other times, she is like a butterfly sampling this pretty flower and that; never still and never willing to be directed.

A child has a different sense of time and priorities from an adult, and the working man finds it very hard to enter into this time. Many fathers discover a real sense of failure here. The temptation is always to try to direct the child's play "Look, build up these two towers of bricks and then we can make a bridge so that Teddy can walk from this one to that one. No, don't knock it down. No..." In the traditional role division it is the father who takes the lead in broadening the child's horizons, and this is still true of most fathers today. Clearly, there is a need for a child to be stretched, so that she may be made aware of new possibilities. The trap so many men fall into, even when aware of it, is never being able to give up their control and surrender themselves to the child.

There are exceptions. Jim works as a management consultant. His job involves a great deal of planning, analysing and directing. Yet he doesn't find the adjustment to his one-year-old son's rhythm of play at all difficult. In fact, he welcomes the change of pace. Playing with Tony and immersing himself in Tony's world is Jim's way of unwinding after coming home from work. Jim is one of the lucky ones; most fathers do not find it so easy. It takes time to get to know a child and to be able to switch into his way of behaving — especially when he can't talk. Many working fathers simply don't have long enough. By the time they've got home, unwound from the cares of the day, and relaxed enough to start accepting a different set of priorities, it will be past bedtime.

Unless they are like Jim, the only way most committed fathers can get close to their children is by spending more time with them. But work also takes up time, energy, and commitment. The conflict often means that one or other has to go. Many fathers find that, because they feel impelled to give priority to work they 'fail' as active and committed fathers. So they give up, and devote ever more energy to a career and a chance of 'success'. So his fatherhood becomes ever more traditional in practice, even if he is still committed to a more active theory of fatherhood.

Perhaps it is simply impossible to have commitment to both home and work, but that is what many men now want. At last there are now some indications that society is gradually changing working practices to allow this to become just a little easier.

The first such change, paternity leave, isn't just of interest to the active father. A survey by the Equal Opportunities Commission in the UK found that 91% of the men interviewed thought there should be some provision for paternity leave around the time of the birth of a baby.

The 5% of men who were definitely against paternity leave tended to have two or more children, to be older than average and to have non-manual jobs. Most of them were able to take time off work without loss of pay. One said, "I wouldn't readily agree with it — it would be open to abuse and would cost a lot of money. It's a sorry tale if you can't find time in your holiday leave to save for this time of birth." In fact many workers, especially manual workers, are not able to take their holiday leave whenever they need it, and it seems fair to say that, apart from these few well-off exceptions, paternity leave appeals just as much to the traditional father as to the more active one.

The most common reason given for wanting paternity leave was "the need to look after your wife and child". The need to give emotional support was also mentioned by several fathers in the sample:

> What I've noticed — after the first two she had depression, really bad but this time since I've been home she's been great — I think it's directly due to me being at home. I've been waiting for the crunch to come but this time she's been really great. I can't see any reason other than me being here to explain it. (*Bell et al*, p.67)

Men with more than one child were particularly insistent on the need for paternity leave. The birth of a second child is often a very stressful time for the father — especially if he hasn't been very involved in the family until then. He can be thrown together with his older child and forced to care for her in a more intensive way than ever before. Many men find that this is the first time they really get to know their older children. Provided the stress is managed properly it can be a positive and rewarding experience for both father and child.

Paternity leave can also be useful in giving the new father a chance to get used to the changes in his life.

> It gives the new father the chance to adjust to this new thing. Those first few weeks of having this new babe around you get very little sleep, you're not a lot of use for anything and I think it would give you the chance to adjust to this, to get the routine settled and actually start sort of becoming a human being again and not a nappy changing zombie. (*Andy*)

Many employers are reluctant to grant paternity leave — especially paid leave. But perhaps they should think more carefully. As men get more involved in pregnancy, birth, and the early weeks after birth it will take them longer to regain their equilibrium. Many men feel that the process would be helped by a period of leave — two weeks is the most commonly quoted figure, but some want six weeks or more — to be taken soon after the baby is born. From an employer's point of view a 'nappy changing zombie' may not be the most reliable or efficient of employees. Looked at in this way, paternity leave may be just as useful to employer as employee.

So far the kind of paternity leave discussed has been fairly small scale and of relevance to almost all fathers. Recently, a proposal for *parental leave* has been discussed in the European Economic Community. This would allow an employed parent the chance to stay at home and take sole or principal care of his or her child after maternity leave had finished. An important thing about these proposals is that an employed father or mother could only take parental leave if he or she had a partner who was also in work. The proposal is for a minimum of three months leave per worker per child. So in a two-parent family the mother could take three months leave while the father worked, and then he could take three months while she worked. This leave would have to be taken before the child was two.

Several countries in the EEC already have some form of parental leave and the Community proposals are, in part, designed to harmonize the different provisions.[24] The public sector is relatively enlightened, but private firms are also gradually coming round to the idea of parental leave.

Several British banks now offer quite generous parental leave to some employees. One of the largest, the Midland, has recently instituted a scheme which allows up to five years unpaid parental leave. This is not open to all employees, but only to 'career bankers' in whom the bank has already invested a lot of resources. Anyone taking up the scheme is guaranteed reappointment on the same grade as the one they held when leaving — although there is no guarantee that they will get exactly the same job back. Pension rights are frozen, and they will be able to go back into the pension without penalty — except for the five fewer years benefit. So far, it has been mostly women who have taken up the offer, but men are also beginning to be included.

The most famous example of parental leave comes from Sweden, where it has been available since 1975. Parents are entitled to up to twelve months parental benefit which they can divide between them as they wish, although only one parent can be on leave at a time. This is in addition to two months antenatal maternity leave and ten days paternity leave. There is no separate postnatal maternity leave. When the scheme started the period of leave was only six months and only 3% of fathers took advantage of their rights. An extra six months was introduced in 1978, and by 1981 22% of men took at least some parental leave (in addition to paternity leave) during the first year of their child's life. The average length of time taken by men was 47 days, which is quite high when you consider that any postnatal maternity leave must be taken from the parental leave. Payment of 90% of gross income is given for the first nine months parental leave, and a basic flat rate for the last three months.

Swedish parents are also entitled to time off to care for a sick child. Relatively few fathers seem to have used this option, but attitudes are changing. In a recent survey, only half of men in their 50s and 60s felt that caring for a sick child was a legitimate reason for taking time off work, while 80% of men aged around 25 felt it to be valid.[25] Similar figures are found in respect of paternity leave: the older the man, the less likely he was to take paternity leave. Sweden is usually ahead of the rest of the world in its social provision, but we tend to catch up in the end. The will for paternity leave and parental leave already exists; how long it takes depends on how much fuss individual men are prepared to make. Some employers and unions are already taking it seriously, but many still do not. Paternity leave is often put on the negotiating table as a hostage to fortune. It is something both sides are prepared to give up in order to achieve what they see as more important goals. The more pressure there is on them, the more likely they are to take it seriously.

Some men are trying other ways of combining work and home. An obvious way of doing this is for both parents to work part-time and be at home part-time, but it has many pitfalls. George and Miranda wanted very much to share the care of their daughter. George was working in a hostel after Samantha was born, and he arranged with them that he and Miranda could share his job. But the pay wasn't very good and they decided to look elsewhere. Eventually they got a job with a local authority with a commitment to jobsharing schemes. This, too, was not a great success and neither of them was happy with the job — both feeling that they were not being stretched or used to their full ability. They decided to try again, but without success. The only solution seemed to be to apply for full-time jobs; the first one to be successful would go out to work, and the other would stay at home with Samantha.

In the event, it was George who got the job. He had been doing it for six months when I last spoke to him. He enjoys it very much and feels that at last his talents are being used. Miranda is not so happy. She feels that she has been pushed back into a traditional mothering role, and this frustrates her. George, too, feels that he is losing touch with Samantha. Neither of them wants Samantha looked after by a nanny or childminder, so they really have few options left. George sees their present position as temporary. They hope to have another child soon, and then he says he will be quite happy to stay at home full-time with the children while Miranda goes out to work. Yet this is not their ideal solution either. They want to share work and home life, but so this has not been possible.

If George does eventually look after the children full-time he will join the ranks of the news-worthy *role-swappers*, so popular with the mass media. Yet his predicament shows how complex such decisions really are. Just because a man stays at home full-time with his children does not mean that his commitment is to full-time fatherhood. He may want to share care, but find himself forced into the situation; he may desperately want a full-time job but be unable to get one; or he may simply have drifted into it as Simon did.

Simon was unhappy with his job, and since Nancy was earning good money they decided that he should give it up and spend time renovating the house. When that was done Simon still didn't want to go back to paid employment, so he used his skills in the community, helping the elderly with small maintainance tasks. When Nancy got pregnant it was sensible that they should continue the arrangement, and that Simon should look after Wayne full-time while she returned to work. They are both reasonably happy with their lifestyle, experiencing many of the same satisfactions and

frustrations as a couple with a more conventional arrangement.

The role-swap is still relatively rare. A recent American survey found only 4 men out of 3600 who were caring for their children full-time. But those men who choose to spend the major part of their middle years caring for children are like the yeast in the dough; whether they like it or not they are hacking a trail through the dense prejudice (both male and female) which has trapped men for so long. The man who willingly stays at home to look after his children is challenging society's view of male and female roles. In 1974, men's magazines such as *Playboy*, *Penthouse*, and *Esquire* ran a two page advertisement for a men's cologne, made by the Scandinavian manufacturer, Scannon Corporation. They showed a rugged Norwegian holding a baby. The caption read, "*Kanon*. Brought to you from the country where men are so sure of themselves, some of them stay home to care for the children". Even one sucessful 'male mother' calls into question many of our folk views about the 'maternal instinct' or the nature of sex roles.

Graham is one example. He and Judy made the decision that he would stay at home to look after their new baby when Judy was four months pregnant:

> The reasons for our decision were many and varied: reasons which by themselves would probably not have had such a dramatic effect, but in combination were irresistible.
>
> a) Judy was really enjoying her job whereas I had been having a series of rows with my boss which eventually made my position untenable.
>
> b) Judy was earning more money than I was and, with her as a computer analyst and myself as a civil engineer this was unlikely to change.
>
> c) The tax situation in the UK was beneficial since the household is taxed as an entity. If a woman gives up work her tax allowance is lost to the household, but a man keeps his. (This anomaly will no doubt be sorted out in the future!)
>
> d) We had realized while we were still engaged and discussing the idea of children that I would probably make a better parent than Judy since, as a Scout leader, I had actually been trained and enjoyed dealing with children. Also I had more patience. It is a question of gifts in the Christian sense — some fathers do make better parents.
>
> e) We foresaw big problems with evening activities. I enjoyed going out and doing things, Judy was more of a back-room person. We felt

that Judy would complain less if I went out in the evening having looked after Margaret during the day. In a sense I have more freedom as a result because I don't feel guilty about it!

f) We wanted to bring up our own children, and there is now an ethical question as to whether it is right to have more than one wage-earner in a household in a country with over three million unemployed.

Graham continued to work until Margaret was almost five months old. Then, after one week's handover, Judy went back to work and Graham was on his own. Judy was still breastfeeding and the plan was for him to feed Margaret with her expressed breast milk, using a bottle. However, Margaret refused to drink from the bottle and had to be fed from a trainer beaker which was a slow process, each feed taking over an hour. Apart from this, Graham experienced no more child care problems than any other parent might expect.

When Judy became pregnant again, Graham went back to work while she was on maternity leave. He didn't really enjoy it and looked forward eagerly to returning to the house. Again Judy went back to work five months after their second daughter was born. Graham was confident that he would be able to cope well, but things didn't work out as he had anticipated. The first month was really bad and the extra strain brought on diabetes. "I had to come to the realization that I wasn't coping. I just wasn't as competent as I thought I was. The funny thing was that as soon as I faced up to this, things became much easier." Graham is now coping well with the two girls and is very happy at home with them. His diabetes has stabilized and is controllable with pills. Despite the bad patch, he is still much happier at home, and would not go back to work unless absolutely necessary.

George and Miranda, and Graham and Judy each chose a different approach to the problem of work and parenting, and each for different reasons. The fact that their solutions are still relatively uncommon masks a more radical and widespread change which has occurred over the last few years — and that is the existence of the choice itself. Fourteen years ago, when Shirley and I decided to have a child, we did not discuss the question of who should work and who stay at home. Even though she was earning more than me, and perhaps had better job prospects than I had, there was no question of me staying at home and her staying at work. It simply wasn't on the agenda. Now, for a small but increasing number of couples, the question is raised and discussed. At a recent antenatal class one couple out of seven had decided that the father would stay at home full-time, and another couple had still not made up their minds.

That is the positive side of the coin. Some couples are beginning to recognize the strains between working and parenting and are trying to deal creatively with them. The negative side is that it is only the favoured few who able to make such choices. Economics still plays a vital role in any such discussion. Many couples, especially those on low incomes, have no such options. They have no chance of a job share because they need two incomes just to survive. Most employers feel threatened by any attempt at more flexible working arrangements. Trade unions are also suspicious, seeing them as a threat to traditional employment practices. Until recently, job sharing has been seen principally as a means of giving women more equal access to the marketplace, while still allowing them to have babies and young children. Men are at last also beginning to recognize the opportunities which job sharing can offer them.[26]

Working practices may change. The spread of computerization and information technology is likely to provide new opportunities for mixing home and work. In 1986 a study undertaken for the British National Economic Development Office predicted that by 1995 over three million Britons could be working from home on computer networks, and that the number may have risen to five million by 2010. Others remain sceptical about the scale of any such changes. It is too early to say what our future work patterns might be; whether there will be a more equal spread of work and home opportunities for all, or whether we will have a small elite of workers; with the majority unemployed, poor and disillusioned. Those few couples who are currently experimenting with new ways of coping with the demands of work and home may be more influential than they realize.

In the meantime, most men are faced with a dilemma. However much they want to compromise, sooner or later they find themselves faced with a choice between work and home. The attractions of career and traditional male values are very strong. The question is, can the pull of home and involvement with the children prove strong enough to overcome the lure of the world of work?

10. Mummies and Daddies

Many couples are quite unprepared for the impact parenthood will make on their lives, both as individuals and as a partnership. Airline pilots spend hours in a simulator in order to perform a task which is infinitely less complex than caring for children. The new mother and father are dropped in at the deep end without anyone enquiring if they even know how to swim.

It is not only the experience of parenthood which is a closed book before birth; the sheer quantity of life that it takes up is also a shock. As part of my work on the Open University's *The First Years of Life*,[27] I asked Jackie and Michael how they thought their lives would be affected if they were to have a baby. Firstly I got them to list the various roles they played in their lives, and then to draw a pie chart showing how they all fitted together. The more important the role, the greater the slice of the pie it should have. It isn't simply a case of how much time is spent on a particular role, but rather how crucial a part it plays in your hopes, desires and priorities.

Jackie and Michael have been living together for a couple of years. They are not married, but Jackie bracketed together her *friend* and *lover* roles as making up a *wife*. She sees her most important role as being *worker* with *wife* coming next. Michael's job — he is a public service worker — is not so important to him. Instead he sees his principal role as creating a home, and spends a lot of time decorating and renovating their new house. Michael and Jackie are not intending to have a baby in the next year or so, but they both want children at some time in their lives.

I then got them to draw a pie chart of how they thought their roles

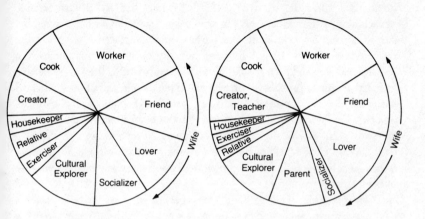

Before Parenthood   After Parenthood

JACKIE'S
CHART

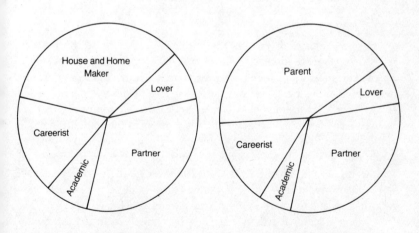

Before Parenthood   After Parenthood

MICHAEL'S
CHART

would look after the birth of a baby. Michael had a fairly reasonable expectation of the amount his life would be changed: *parent* is by far the largest slice in his new chart. But he has simply replaced *house and home maker* with *parent* as if the two were mutually exclusive. This allows him to keep his *lover* and *partner* roles almost as important as they were before. In practice, things probably won't be as simple as this, but at least Michael has some idea of the size of the change. Jackie's expectations of the impact of a baby on her life seem less realistic. Although she realizes that her social life will be cut down, she actually anticipates an increase in her role as a *lover*. Jackie's expectation of the *parent* segment is so small that, if she were to have a baby now, she would probably experience severe distress because of her lack of preparation.

The new role, *mother* or *father*, must be slotted in somewhere, and this has two major repercussions for the new parents. Firstly it means that the individual has to reorganize his or her personal priorities in order to accommodate the new responsibilities. Secondly, the couple have to reorganize their relationship. Before the birth they interacted with each other on the basis of the expectations each had of the other's roles and the rights and duties associated with those roles. When the roles themselves change in nature and importance the relationship itself has to be re-negotiated.

In this adjustment process the traditional father has distinct advantages over his more involved counterparts. He is more likely to belong to a close-knit network of friends and workmates who will not only provide help and comfort, but also exert quite a strong influence by guiding him towards appropriate role behaviour. In any case, the traditional father will have to make less of a change in his behaviour than the committed father. He will already be giving high priority to work, and will probably have a traditional set of attitudes towards the division of labour in the home. His partner is likely to share his views and rely on her network for support, rather than on him. The effect of the new baby will be to reinforce these network ties, and to underpin the values of traditional fatherhood.

Many traditional fathers now get very involved in pregnancy and birth — especially birth — and want to spend time with their partner and baby immediately after the birth. But as soon as the traditional father returns to work he is pulled towards a more 'old-fashioned' kind of fatherhood. He may, in fact, hardly be aware of the changes which are occurring. Traditional family patterns have great survival value and as long as both partners are happy with their separate parental roles they should be able to adjust to the new baby fairly easily. It will be hard work of course, but they won't have to undergo radical changes of self-image, or need to work out the practical implications of a new set of ideals and values.

It's not so simple for the active father. He has the same practical difficulties as the traditional father, but in addition he has to work out the details of his new involvement in child care. Most active fathers spend at least some part of the week in sole or principal charge of their children. Graeme Russell has documented the pressures which this can put on the marital relationship. He discovered that marital satisfaction was lower for couples who shared care than for those in traditional families. In particular the shared care couples were more likely to have considered ending their relationship, left the house recently after a quarrel, felt the relationship wasn't going well, and felt that they got on each other's nerves.

Graeme Russell's sample included both men who wanted to share care, and those who found themselves forced into it because of economic circumstances. They were therefore not all 'active fathers' in the sense that I use the term. He did find slight indications that those who were keen to share were more satisfied with the marriage than those who had no choice, but this difference was not very significant. Even the active fathers found it much more of a strain than the fathers in traditional families.

Despite his difficulties, the active father does at least know what he is aiming for. His goals are high involvement in child care, and equality in the decision making and responsibilities of the home; and even if these are hard to achieve he can usually judge how well he is doing. The man I have characterized as the 'committed father' is not so clear about his role. He tries to compromise between home and work, and may well feel that it is wrong to define fatherhood or motherhood too closely. He knows that he is supposed to be more involved in child care than the traditional father, but doesn't know how *much* involvement is required, or of what kind. To some, this new flexibility is a positive advantage. Parents writing about mothers' and fathers' roles came up with the following comments:

> Conventionally the mother makes all the main decisions about a child's welfare — but this should change. Obviously the mother has the main links in early days via breastfeeding — a greater opportunity for bonding. Mother has to handle the shift of emphasis from partner to child; the (conventional) father feels left out. (New style father, being equally involved and very understanding, gives and receives affection equally.) (*father*)

> There must be one parent who is primarily concerned with child care

— which one doesn't matter, but the partner concerned should be consistent — either mother or father. (*mother*)

I want to suggest that we shouldn't be expecting mothers and fathers to have pre-defined roles: individuals differ in what they can offer a child. What that may be will initially be determined by our own upbringing but might, in the long term, depend more on our individual personalities. (*father*)

A free-wheeling creative approach to parental roles is attractive in theory and exciting in practice — as long as things go well. In times of crisis or self-doubt it can be harder to sustain. With clearly defined roles it is easier to see how closely you fit in with your own, and society's, expectations. If there are no clear guidelines you've got to make up your own. There are times when this is relatively easy, and by far the most palatable option. But at times of rapid change or great stress the lack of clear boundaries and directions can easily add to your problems, and give you just one more thing to think and worry about.

In the last chapter I looked at the pressures of work for the committed father. But he has a further problem: not only is he to be more involved in the home, he also has to *share*. 'Sharing' is the committed father's version of equality in the home. It differs from genuine equality in several ways, and is a very slippery concept. To illustrate it more clearly, and to show some of the problems the committed father may run into I present a scenario which shows 'sharing' in action. In fact this kind of scene needn't involve children, and some couples may have played this game before becoming parents.

Joseph and Elizabeth have been married for nine years. Joseph works full-time and Elizabeth has just started a part-time job. They have two children — Susan, aged seven and Bobby, aged five. It is Sunday morning and Joseph is sitting down after breakfast reading the newspaper. Elizabeth comes into the room. "Anything I can do to help, dear?" asks Joseph.

"No thank you" says Elizabeth as she goes into the kitchen.

Joseph continues to read the paper. Half an hour later Elizabeth re-appears. "How long until dinner?" he asks.

"I don't know." she replies, "But I can tell you one thing. It would have been ready a good deal sooner if you'd got off your backside and helped me!"

Joseph is hurt and surprised. "What do you mean? I asked if there was anything I could do, and you said there wasn't."

"Why do you have to ask? Use your initiative for goodness sake! You manage to make decisions at the office, so why do suddenly turn into a wimp when you walk through the front door? I've got better things to do with my time than tell you what needs to be done around the place. Just use your eyes!" The door slams so hard that Joseph thinks his first job will have to be to replace the hinges. For of course he is now stung into action. He will use his eyes, and his initiative. Twenty minutes later he walks into the kitchen, where Elizabeth is now preparing lunch, carrying an armful of sheets. "There you are. That's one job you won't have to do."

"What have you done?" Somehow she doesn't seem as pleased as Joseph thought she would be. (Deep down he knew that she wouldn't like it, but he didn't dare admit that even to himself.) "Don't tell me you've changed the beds? Oh no! I always do that on Wednesdays; they didn't need doing today."

"Well, you won't have to do it on Wednesday, will you?" he says defensively.

"But what about the washing? Now I'll have to wash them today, and that just means more work. I can't do it now or the dinner will spoil so I'll have to spend this afternoon doing it. I was going to have a rest." A new thought suddenly strikes her, "Which sheets did you put on Susan's bed?"

"The blue ones. Why?"

"Oh you idiot! The yellow ones are hers. She'll go spare if she finds out. You must have seen the blue sheets on Bobby's bed a hundred times. Don't you know anything that goes on in this house?" "Look, I'm sorry. I wasn't thinking. I'll change the sheets over, and I'll wash these dirty ones too. You won't have to do a thing."

Elizabeth doesn't speak; her look says it all. Nevertheless it seems that Joseph has retrieved the situation somewhat. Alas, the worst is yet to come.

Joseph takes the dirty clothes to the washing machine. "Darling, what setting should I use? And how much powder should I put in?"

It is the last straw. "Just put them on the floor and leave it to me!" she screams. "It's just so much easier to do it myself. Go away, carry on reading your paper. I'll call you when the dinner is ready."

Joseph retires abjectly. He's not even quite sure what has been going on. Clearly he was in the wrong when he didn't help (or was he?), but surely he was in the right when he did help (or was he?). It had been a very confusing morning. In future he'd just keep his head down and let her get on with it.

This scene never actually occurred. Not in that exact form, anyway. But variations on the theme have been performed in countless venues throughout the Western world. Many of the men and women I have shared it with have recognized themselves in it. They know the ending even before I tell it.

It shows the way the committed father makes problems as well as encountering them. Elizabeth's point about initiative and decision making was straight to the point. Many men fail to accept responsibility in the home, even when they are prepared to help with the housework or child care. How, one might ask, could a man be married for nine years and still not be able to operate a washing machine? But, believe me, it can happen. However, instead of looking at the problems the committed father makes for himself (and for his partner of course), I want to concentrate on the problems that he has.

It is a question of power. For many years women have wielded power in the home. Even if the overt authority belonged to the male 'head of the household', in the majority of cases it was the women who made the important practical domestic decisions. You have only to consider the stereotype of the Jewish or Italian mother or the supposedly matriarchal nature of American family life to see how pervasive the power of the mother in the home can be. As a result, women have tended to identify the domestic sphere as their particular area of competence just as men have tended to identify themselves with their work. A 'good' woman and 'proper' mother is one who performs the household and child care tasks effectively and efficiently. Since many of these tasks are boring and unpleasant, it is not surprising that women should want help from their menfolk. But *help* is all they need. Many women want to keep control over the house for themselves.

So the committed father who feels that he ought to be involved around the house is often denied any real opportunity to participate, except on his partner's terms. Further, many men lack knowledge of basic housework skills because of their upbringing by women, their mothers. Stuart came across this ambivalence when he was out with his eighteen-month-old daughter:

We go to this toddler group and one woman was sitting there complaining about her husband not doing any work around the house, and the next minute she was telling her son off for playing with an ironing board, a wee toy ironing board. I was amazed, I mean I thought that was ridiculous.

The distribution of power in a household used to be more clearly defined than it is now. Today it often has to be negotiated in encounters like the one between Joseph and Elizabeth. If they are to resolve their problem then both will have to change. He must learn to take responsibility and acquire the appropriate skills, and she must be prepared to give up power and share her knowledge with him. It is Elizabeth who holds the upper hand in this situation. She has control of the housework and if she will not relinquish some of it their tensions will continue, or else Joseph will have to revert to a more traditional role.

Scenarios like this have been analysed before, from a woman's point of view, and not surprisingly rather different conclusions have been drawn. For instance, Pat Mainardi presents and interprets several male responses to housework, drawn from her own experiences with her husband:

> *I don't mind sharing the work, but you'll have to show me how to do it.*
>
> Meaning: I ask a lot of questions and you'll have to show me everything, every time I do it because I don't remember so good. Also, don't try to sit down and read while I'm doing my jobs because I'm going to annoy hell out of you until it's easier to do it yourself.
>
> *I've got nothing against sharing the housework, but you can't make me do it on your schedule.*
>
> Meaning: Passive resistance. I'll do it when I damn well please, if at all. If my job is doing dishes, it's easier to do them once a week. If taking out laundry, once a month. If washing the floors, once a year. If you don't like it, do it yourself oftener, and then I won't do it at all.

And so on... She is right of course; many (most? all?) men use the fact of women's domestic power and greater expertise to try to opt out of housework. But this does not diminish the fact that many (most? all?) women gain satisfaction from the exercise of this power and find it a tempting weapon to use in domestic politics.

The figures I obtained from the questionnaires I referred to in chapter one give some indication of the complexity of the relationship between housework and parenting. Most women give it a low priority and hence a low status. Nevertheless, almost a third of those asked thought that it was more important to motherhood than fatherhood (and they were not necessarily the ones who scored it high). The committed father thinks that, in theory at least, doing housework is an important part of being a father; so he feels he ought to be involved in it — even though he doesn't really want to do it. His partner feels that his level of involvement ought to be lower than hers, while at the same time she wants to keep her own involvement as low as possible, which means that he must do more to help, and so on. Confused? Join the club! This conflict of priorities is both an expression and a consequence of the present parental role uncertainty, and makes it even harder to come to a reasonable compromise.[28]

Having disagreements about housework is an example of *Mummies and Daddies*. Children play this game as a way of preparing themselves for adulthood. Grown-ups play it too, as a way of defining their roles as parents. At its best, it can be a creative way of redistributing power and responsibility in the home. At its worst, when played for keeps, it can lead to distress and divorce. Mummies and Daddies isn't just about housework; it can be played in other ways too:

It is a Saturday afternoon. Helen is watching television, Tim is doing the crossword, and Simon, who is five, is playing with modelling clay. Helen looks up.

"Oh Simon, you've dropped a bit on the floor. Pick up will you dear, before it gets trodden into the carpet."

"In a minute Mum. When I've finished making this dinosaur."

"Do it now, please, Simon."

The change in her tone makes Tim look up from his newspaper. He glances round the room before returning to his deliberations about 15 down (*Put a fishy top in a different way to find a father's duty*). He's been staring at it for five minutes now, but he still can't make head nor tail of it. Simon grins at his mother and then continues with his modelling. A pity. He has misjudged her mood.

"Simon, if you don't pick that up right now, you'll go to your room."

"Oh Mum, just let me finish."

"No. Do it *now*."

Simon sets his jaw, glares at Helen, and does not move. Tim glances up, and then buries his face even lower into the newspaper. He can't seem to concentrate on that clue.

"Alright, that's it. Go to your room now. Go on!"

Simon's face crumples into tears and he rushes from the room. Helen, furious, turns on Tim.

"Thank you very much, Tim." She doesn't mean it. "That's just typical of you; leaving me to deal with that scene all by myself. You never back me up. When are you going to start taking some responsibility for your children?"

She sweeps out of the room, leaving Tim feeling confused and guilty. What had he done wrong? His eye falls on the crossword again. Of course! A 'fishy top' is 'piscine lid' and that's an anagram of ... *discipline*.

It is a Saturday afternoon. Helen is watching television, Tim is doing the crossword and Simon, who is an artistic though untidy child, is painting. Helen looks up.

"Simon dear, don't swirl the water around like that. You'll spill it."

Simon is afflicted with temporary deafness. One of its side effects is that his hand gyrates ever faster.

"Simon!"

The change in tone alerts Tim. He looks up from his consideration of fifteen down (*Seat, back and legs in the new order tell fathers what they must not be*). It is the mark of intelligence to learn from past experiences. Tim thinks he is intelligent.

"Simon, you heard what your mother said. Stop sloshing that water about."

The hand wavers for an instant, then resolutely continues.

"Simon, I won't tell you again."

"But Dad, if I don't stir it round properly the brush won't come clean and it will spoil the colour and..."

"Right, you've had your chance. Go to your room, right now."

Surprise, then anger overtakes Simon. He slams the paintbrush down on the table and then rushes to the door.

"And don't you dare slam that..." SLAM! "...door!"

In the gaping silence that follows, Helen turns slowly to Tim.

"Thank you very much, Tim." She still doesn't mean it. "Why did you have to interfere like that? Everything was perfectly under control until you butted in. Trust you to make a mountain out of a molehill! In future, when I start something, just let me finish it in my own way."

Helen doesn't slam the door as she leaves. She has too much style for that, and the effect is much more devastating. Tim sinks back into his chair. Wrong again; he should have stayed with the crossword. Where was he? Oh yes, fifteen down. Well, its obvious now. 'Seat, back and legs' are all 'chair parts' and that's an anagram of ... *patriarchs*.

It is a Saturday afternoon. Helen is doing the crossword. She has come to the conclusion that there is more to crossword puzzles than meets the eye. Tim has decided that writing silly words in little boxes is a pointless and puerile occupation. He is watching the television. There is a kind of quiz show on. The contestants have to work out the title of a book or film by guessing some cryptic clues. This one seems to have some connection with what fishermen do. Simon, who is an artistic and untidy (though stubborn) child, is cutting out pictures and pasting them into his scrapbook. Tim looks up. Quick Tim! Be decisive; don't wait for Helen to take the initiative.

"Simon, do be careful with that glue. It's going everywhere. Just keep it on the paper."

But what's the point in that? There's no fun in being careful, certainly not when you're five. And anyway, *some* of the glue is going on the pictures. Simon continues with studied abandon. The second part of the book title in the TV quiz appears to concern the number of points you need to bust in blackjack. Tim, confused, notices that Simon's activity continues anabated.

"Simon, what did I just tell you? If you don't keep the glue on the paper, you'll have to stop." Strange to relate, Simon doesn't manage to control his pasting, Tim doesn't manage to control his temper, the situation escalates from minor skirmish to major battle and ends in the inevitable exit and slam of door. Helen now breaks her silence. She rounds on Tim.

"What on earth was all that for? All the kid was doing was making a little mess. He's only five, for goodness sake! You've got to make allowances and give him some freedom to explore his creativity, not jump down his throat at the slightest excuse. I'm really fed up with your heavy handedness!"

> As she sweeps from the room, Tim numbly hears the answer to the
> quiz show connundrum. The title of the book was, of course ... *Catch
> 22*.

Discipline is always a problem for parents. The concept itself is a slippery
one. When I have spoken to parents about discipline, it is clear that some
make a big distinction between discipline and obedience to authority, while
others see the two as almost synonomous. In the traditional family
structure the mother would be responsible for day-to-day disciplinary
measures, while the father would remain the ultimate source of authority.
Today most mothers regard the chilling phrase, 'Wait till your father gets
home' as an admission of failure. They feel they should be competent to
deal with all the traumas of the day by themselves, rather than having to
rely on the heavy hand of the paterfamilias when he eventually gets home.
There is also a widespread belief that if punishment has to be handed out,
it should be given as soon as possible after an offence. This, too, has led
to the lessening of the use of the absent father as a threat.

Men have welcomed the change. It may be part of the 'flight from
responsibility' which Barbara Ehrenreich has charted, but many are happy
to relinquish the role of ogre. One of the problems experienced by the
more active father is that he has to get more involved in the dirty work of
discipline. As one Australian father said to Graeme Russell:

> It has increased both the amount of pleasure and the amount of pain
> that I get from my children. I always seem to be nagging them to
> do something — this was something I never did before. They give
> you so many day-to-day problems — fighting, falling over and so
> on ... I really enjoy the break from them now. (p.123)

The active father may not like it, but he has no choice. Other fathers are
making a conscious effort to avoid situations where they might end up
being feared rather than loved. The committed father, in particular, finds it
very difficult to set the level of his authority and control over his children.
Although he recognizes the practical necessity, he often has a set of ideals
which tell him that they ought to be dispensed with. The dilemma can
easily freeze him into inaction or irrational over-reaction.

Many men now seem to put great stress on the concept of being
'friends' with their children. This, too, may be an aspect of their new desire
to create a good relationship with the children. Charlie Lewis found that
the men in his survey were less likely to think of their children as 'naughty'
than their wives were. They were also more likely to want to pick them

"I don't care if you are its father. Only mothers allowed here!"

up if they cried. The Victorian stereotype has been reversed: once it was the father who was the stern parent, now he is soft and indulgent.

As women become more assertive and confident of their own authority, and men become less so, discipline becomes one of the key areas for domestic encounter. One of the most common complaints I hear from women today is that their husbands are 'opting out of discipline'. They may be right, but this is largely because an increasing number of men now feel that they are in a no-win game and the only way to survive is to stop playing. The committed father runs into trouble in the home because he intrudes on the female domain which his partner has carved out for herself. He can run into similar difficulties outside the home.

It is not until they become fathers that most men experience sexism directly; that is, prejudice against them simply on grounds of their sex. But once a man embarks on fatherhood for the first time he will be lucky to escape it. Firstly, there is institutional prejudice: in the antenatal clinic where he may be ignored, in the antenatal class where he may be matronized, in the labour room where he may be treated as an irrelevance, and in the postnatal ward where he may be treated as an inconvenience. Many men have been shocked and surprised to be on the receiving end of such treatment. Yet the majority accept it as normal and don't question it unless they are given a specific opportunity.

Let me give an example. A constant problem for parents is what to do if your baby needs to be fed or changed while you are out shopping. Good changing facilities are rare, but in 1985 a scheme was launched in Britain which tries to improve things. Selected establishments now display a *Baby Care Symbol*. It started life as an idea for a breastfeeding symbol which would indicate places where a mother could breastfeed her baby, but the scheme was eventually broadened to include changing rooms "for mothers and their children which provide cleanliness, warmth, seating, privacy and washing facilities with paper towels and a waste bin". The symbol is sponsored both by health professionals and by consumer groups such as the National Childbirth Trust and La Leche League, and its launch was supported by the Mothercare chain of maternity stores.

Unfortunately, the exclusiveness of the phrase *mothers and their children* is not just a slip of the pen — as Jim discovered. When his son, Andy, was eight months old Jim and Amy decided to swap roles. One day, when Jim was out shopping, Andy needed a clean nappy. While Jim was in Mothercare he noticed one of the new Baby Care Symbols. The shop was empty and no-one was using the changing facilities. This was clearly the solution to his problem. He walked towards the changing room, only to be stopped by the assistant who told him that he couldn't go in, because the facilities were only for women. Jim asked why, but could get no other answer. She just continued to repeat that the facilities were only for women. In the end Jim walked half a mile back to his car, changed Andy, and then walked half a mile back into the city centre to continue his shopping. Jim told me, "I was very annoyed. If it had been a male assistant I think I would have lost my cool, but as it was I just walked out the shop. I think it's disgusting".

This isn't the only example of discrimination Jim has faced. He wanted to do some weight training at a nearby leisure centre to keep himself in trim. So he tried to arrange it at the same time as the ladies' yoga class for which the centre laid on a crèche. But he was told that the because the crèche was for women with children he would not be able to leave Andy there! Jim's experience is not unique. Every man I know who looks after his children has told me similar stories.

Sometimes the prejudice is personal rather than institutional. Here the rejection is more subtle, but no less hurtful. I remember taking my daughter, Rebecca, to the play centre in the local park (with its big sign which said, *For Mothers and Children Under Five Only*) and feeling totally out of place as the only man present. None of the women spoke to me, nor did there seem to be an opening for me to speak to them. It was a very alienating experience — one I did not repeat. I am actually not very good with strangers, but I have since spoken to so many men who had similar experiences that I am sure that in this instance it wasn't just my shyness, but a real structural problem.

The active father who has sole care of his children during the day cannot adopt the soft option of staying out of women's territory. If he doesn't use the facilities, his children will suffer. So he perseveres, and eventually women will speak freely to him. But before complete acceptance comes (if it ever does) he usually has to put up with a great deal of matronizing behaviour from at least some of those present. It is done under the guise of friendliness, and often is genuinely kind in intention, but the message is cruel: 'You're only a man so you couldn't possibly know how to do that properly. Let me do it for you'. And even when acceptance comes there are still residual doubts.

> All the women are nice to me when I go, and they always make a big fuss of me and "It's nice to see the dads doing the work for a change" and that kind of comment, but I must admit I do feel a bit out of place, standing in a room with thirty women. It's almost as if

you're on exhibition, and everybody's watching you to see if you've
changed the nappy properly, and this kind of thing. (*Ian*)

Fathers experience institutional sexism and personal sexism, both inside and
outside the home. The reasons are many; one of the most important is that
many women feel threatened by the man who has a real commitment to
fathering. Such women define their personhood in terms of their mothering
and housekeeping, just as many men define themselves in terms of work.
They see this as the one area in which they are successful and indeed
superior to men. A man who intrudes onto this territory sets off some
pretty deep-rooted defense mechanisms. She will try to exclude him, or
undermine his confidence, or put him down, or play no-win games with
him.

There are those who believe that only men practice sexism, and that
only women are oppressed because of their gender. Some radical feminists
hold this as a developed theoretical position, but many women simply
accept it without argument. The involved father knows, from personal
experience, that it is not true. The question is, what should he do about it?

There is a temptation to retaliate, to match oppression with anger. It
is possible to make a few cheap debating points by pointing out examples
of women's sexism (I know, I have done it), but it is not a good thing to
do. The way forward does indeed involve exposing prejudice and
oppression whenever it appears, but with understanding and constructive
concern. A certain degree of assertiveness and campaigning may be needed
to break down the kind of structural sexism found in public institutions,
but the only thing that will work in the home is honest analysis and loving
acceptance of the complexity of relationships. Only in such a setting can
the games parents play lead them forward to a greater understanding of
each other.

Committed fathers face opposition from women both in the home and
outside it. Many are unable to cope. They distance themselves from their
homes and from their children, in order to reduce the opportunities for
conflict. But by doing so they also retreat from their earlier high ideals and
drift back towards traditional fatherhood. As they are pushed out of home
and child care, so they are pulled into the world of work and career
prospects. They still believe in the ideals of commitment, involvement, and
power sharing, but the practicalities are just too difficult. It is easier to sink
back into the patterns learned in childhood and abdicate responsibility for
child care, leaving the few active fathers to carry the torch for genuine male
participation in child care.

11. Goodbye Father?

Mark, aged thirteen, was going out for the day with his friends. "Be careful!" said Shirley. "Be good!" said I, under my breath. A small moment, but it summed up one of the deepest differences between traditional mothers and fathers: the emphasis each places on care and control.

It is possible for a man to go through the first quarter of his life without ever really being aware of the existence of children. They are invisible; not a part of his universe at all. The advent of pregnancy changes everything. Suddenly children appear from all directions and their impact is immediate. Partly, of course, this is because he and his partner start seeking out the company of friends or relations who already have children, and partly it is because the changed circumstances have increased his awareness of a part of the world to which he was previously blind.

One thing which usually strikes men very forcefully is how badly most children seem to behave. They are noisy, rude, dirty, uncouth, obtrusive, argumentative, disobedient and desperately in need of discipline. It is at that this point that most of us resolve that our children will not be so naughty; we will insist on proper standards of behaviour. Later on of course, when the reality of having children comes home to us, we may think very differently. We may come to realize the futility of applying adult standards to childish behaviour, or may develop a tolerance and understanding of the child's point of view which is usually totally lacking in the non-father.

Some men are able to cope adequately with the problems of discipline, but most have great difficulties — either being too 'heavy' or else 'opting out', as we saw in the last chapter. There is no doubt that discipline is a more loaded issue for men than for women. Men seem to feel a greater need than women to control their children. I think we also feel a greater sense of hurt and rejection when our children rebel and defy us — even though this is often tempered by a kind of perverse pride at the child's burgeoning independence.

Men certainly tend to react more oppressively than women if faced by a naughty child, insisting on their interpretation, and often seeming unable to accept any compromise. As their children grow up and start to assert themselves, most men are forced to confront a previously undiscovered dark side of the soul. In the cold light of day it can be very painful to think back on the quite unreasonable anger you showed when your child stepped over some trivial and often arbitrary boundary. Indeed, your reaction is often most harsh when the infringement is least serious in real terms.

Why do men have these problems with discipline and control? It appears that there is a universal tendency for men to want to dominate others: women, children, and weaker men — but especially women. In culture after culture we find that women and children have to defer to a male authority figure. This is usually the man who by right of biology or ritual or marriage is identified as their father/husband, but even where the 'father' in this sense has little authority, it will not be the mother who has control but another man — often one of her brothers. There are always *individual* exceptions where a forceful woman will dominate, or even batter, her less forceful husband, but the general social pattern in every culture is of male control.

Some feminist writers have denied that male control, *patriarchy*, is universal. They claim that there are now, or have been in the past, matriarchal societies in which women were pre-eminent. When subjected to critical analysis these claims do not stand up in any meaningful sense. The historical record is uncertain, and the evidence quoted consists largely of legends such as those about the Amazons, a mythical race of warrior women. As far as the present day is concerned, it is true that there are some societies in which women are accorded a revered and important place, but even in these the majority of positions of power and prestige are held by men.

The reason for this universal male dominance is unclear. Some argue that it has a biological basis, others that it is social in origin. The debate about patriarchy and male dominance is itself part of the wider debate about gender roles, and whether these are innate or learned. The evidence is conflicting and often contradictory, and it is hard to be objective about

it. People often adopt a position because it suits their own outlook on life, rather than because the evidence is really overwhelming.

My own view is that the evidence suggests that there are definite biologically based differences between the sexes, which express themselves in tendencies towards different kinds of behaviour (males tend to be dominant, females tend to be nurturant, for instance) but that there is scope for moderating these tendencies by upbringing, and by structuring society in appropriate ways. This middle position is held by most people; the key unanswered question concerns the relative importance of biology versus society — nature versus nurture — as influences on our behaviour.

The relevant evidence comes from both human and non-human studies. For instance, it has been found that if testosterone, a male hormone, is administered to female rabbits during the last twelve days of pregnancy, they are more likely to kill their young or fail to nurse. Female rats which received male hormones at four days after giving birth behaved less maternally (in terms of retrieving, licking and nursing strange pups) than a control group which were not given the hormones. In the same study male rats who were castrated at birth and who could therefore not make testosterone, showed more nurturant behaviour than intact males. This was not true of rats who were castrated when they were 25 days old. Other studies with rats have shown that female rats given doses of male hormones just after birth are also more dominant than ordinary females.

Many researches believe that a lot of the gender behaviour differences between men and women arise because males are exposed to greater amounts of testosterone while they are still in the womb. This happens as the male fetus' own testes develop and start making male hormones. It is claimed that these hormones actually influence the development of the central nervous system in ways which predispose men towards different behaviour from women.

Hard evidence is not easy to find, especially in the case of human beings. Even those who feel that the search for knowledge justifies the practice of castrating rats do not usually advocate such a procedure for humans. There have therefore been no comparable experiments on human mothers or babies. Nevertheless, accidents occur which appear to shed some light on these complex questions. One famous case concerns a young American boy whose penis was destroyed when he was seven months old during an attempt to circumcise him. The physician used an electric cauterizing needle instead of a scalpel, and after a couple of abortive attempts turned the current up so high that he cooked the boy's penis and it subsequently dropped off. Eventually, it was suggested to the distraught parents that the best solution might be to 'reassign' the boy as a girl by removing his testes and constructing female external genitals by plastic surgery. When the child reached the age of puberty s/he would be given female sex hormones to feminize her body.

The parents agreed, and the child was brought up as a girl from the age of fifteen months. She had actually been born as one of twin boys and had been the dominant brother in the early months. Nevertheless, despite the fact that she had been exposed to male sex hormones while in the womb, by the age of five she was able to act as a girl — albeit a rather tomboyish one. Her dominance behaviour changed to 'fussing' over her twin brother, and she became more concerned with clothes and appearance and helping in the kitchen than he was.

This particular case is often cited as showing that the influence of hormones is not as important as the effect of upbringing, but recently it has been suggested that this girl has had great difficulties at puberty and found it hard, if not impossible, to adjust to the notion of being a woman. Perhaps the influence of the early exposure to male hormones is more important than some like to admit.

Additional evidence that this might be the case comes from a family in the Dominican Republic, all descendants of one woman who had an unusual genetic condition. Her genes have been detected in 23 families in three separate villages, and 38 individuals have been directly affected by their inheritance. All of them were born and brought up as girls, and then at puberty changed into boys!

In fact they were genetically male all the time and had undescended testes which were able to produce the male hormone testosterone, but they were not able to process it into another hormone which is responsible for shaping the external male sex organs in the fetus. Because of this the Dominican children were brought up as girls and it came as a complete surprise to all the family when they started developing male sex organs, and had to shave. However, it is reported that none of the children had trouble adjusting to their new lives as men, despite the fact that they were raised as girls. It has been suggested that the fact that they had been exposed to testosterone from their own testes in the womb was a greater influence than their upbringing.[29]

These and other studies suggest that testosterone plays an important part in the creation of sex differences between males and females. It has also been implicated in differences in dominance behaviour. One of the most thorough-going biological theories has been proposed by Stephen Goldberg. He points out that some people say that male dominance is based on the fact that males are stronger and more athletically able than females. However, there is also a strong body of evidence which suggests that women do not feel the same need to dominate as men do. So while physical superiority may be necessary for males to dominate women, it is not of itself a sufficient explanation of *why* men should want to do so. Stephen Goldberg attempts to get round this difficulty by suggesting a biological mechanism which accounts for the differences between men and women.

According to Goldberg, the very universality of patriarchy and male dominance make it almost inevitable that they have some underlying biological basis — otherwise there would be exceptions. He suggests that men are more likely to react with dominance behaviour in a situation of hierarchy because of the influence of male sex hormones — both from the exposure in the womb and from the male's normally higher levels of testosterone. Although there is a great deal of evidence to support this position, it is clear that the theory is a statistical one. It accepts that some women are more dominant than some men. Goldberg also accepts that the way we are brought up — socialization, as the social scientists call it — has some part to play, but as far as he is concerned, all that upbringing can do is to reinforce and make explicit the innate biological tendencies. It is at this point that the weaknesses in his presentation become clear. For instance, he writes:

> Even if it were possible for socialization to ignore the psycho-physiological reality — and for children to be socialized to believe that fathers were not dominant and tall, mothers not nurturant and short — the physiological factors would still be at work and fathers would still be dominant and tall, mothers nurturant and short. (p.104)

There are two points to make here. Firstly, the theory does not maintain that fathers are dominant, but they they have a tendency to dominance. Secondly, height is an attribute which is genetically determined and which cannot be altered except by surgery or accident. A dominance tendency is a behavioural influence which can be changed — unless our actions are completely determined by the action of our hormones. Nevertheless, the implications of Goldberg's theory is clear: fathers will tend to dominate their partners and children.

Assume, for the moment, that Goldberg is right. What are the consequences in human terms? Is this a good state of affairs, or should we be trying to change it? As a beginning, consider the following definition of fatherhood. It says much the same as the cool scientific research findings, but the impact is very different:

> ...we must remember that a father is simply a male who has possession and control of a female (or more than one) and her offspring. (*Rich*, p.67)

Possession and control? Is this, then, the chilling reality of fatherhood? Is this what male dominance means in practice? There are those who believe that it is so. And they have much evidence to support their view. We have already seen that male control seems to be universal, and based on the normal biological differences between men and women. Possession, too, seems to be an almost universal characteristic of fatherhood. "Who giveth this woman to be married to this man?" The famous question from the Prayer Book wedding service requires no spoken answer; what is required is for a man — the bride's father or a substitute for him — to step forward and 'give away' the bride. Perhaps today, for us, this is just a symbolic remnant of an old social order, but there are still many societies where it seems to be literally true. Marriage is a matter decided by two fathers: the prospective bride and groom have nothing to do with it.

In many societies it isn't just a matter of arranging the marriage, nor is the bride 'given away'. Instead she is exchanged, either for another woman ('I'll give my daughter to your family, if your family will give me your daughter as my son's bride') or for some form of bridewealth. There are those who see this as a simple form of ownership: women are owned by their fathers who dispose of them as they see fit, either by selling them for cattle or by swapping them for other women. (Others deny that 'ownership' is involved, preferring to speak of 'control'.)

Fatherhood is seen, in this analysis, as a means by which men exert power over women and children; denying them their rightful freedom. But the indictment of fatherhood does not end here, in the father-dominated family. On the contrary, according to the radical feminists, the relations of dominance and control which men must exercise in order to assert their 'fatherhood' are reproduced and magnified in society as a whole. Where Stephen Goldberg sees patriarchy and male dominance as manifestations of the same biological reality, Adrienne Rich sees patriarchy as fatherhood writ large:

> Patriarchy is the power of the fathers: a familial-social, ideological, political system in which men — by force, direct pressure or through ritual, tradition, law, and language, customs, etiquette, education, and

the division of labor, determine what part women shall or shall not play, and in which the female is everywhere subsumed under the male. (p.57)

According to radical feminism, patriarchy is a means of controlling and oppressing women. It denies women equal access to power and prestige in the world — indeed, our very notions of power and prestige are defined by men, without reference to women. Men even try to control the reproductive power of women — most obstetricians are male, and the increasing presence of men at birth is just one more example of male intrusion into the domain of women's reproduction. Patriarchy is the rule of the female by the male, of the weaker male by the more powerful male. It dehumanizes; treating other people, especially women, as objects to be controlled, used and disposed of as the patriarchs think fit.

Patriarchy achieves its aims by a variety of methods. According to Mary Daly it uses four techniques. Firstly there is the killing of women, as in the witchcraft trials of the Middle Ages, where thousands of women were tortured and killed. Secondly, it rewrites the natural order of things, as when Eve is born from Adam or Athena from Zeus. Thirdly, it tries to redefine and colonize feminism in order to control and manipulate it. And lastly it uses divide and conquer tactics by training 'token' women to operate in patriarchal professions and so dilute the opposition. (*Daly*, 1978, p.8)

For radical feminists such as Kate Millett and Shulamith Firestone, the basis of the subjugation of women is the father-led family. "Patriarchy's chief institution is the family." says Kate Millett (p.33). Shulamith Firestone followed this up and suggested that the liberation of women required them to be freed from family structures, and the dependence on men that the facts of birth and childcare forced upon them. According to Firestone, the new reproductive technologies of artificial insemination and *in vitro* fertilization now offer the hope of liberation from the ties of biology and the oppression of men.

Others, such as Susan Brownmiller, claim that the basis of patriarchy is not the family, but male violence — especially the actuality and the fear of rape. In a sense it matters little whether it is the power of the father or the fear of rape. Domination by physical and psychological means is both the cause and the effect of patriarchy. Rape and family structure are in any case intimately connected. In many Western countries it is not possible, legally, for a man to rape his wife. The law grants him unlimited sexual access to her. Whether or not rape is the cause of patriarchy, it is its archetypal expression. If fatherhood is responsible for the creation of rapists then perhaps fatherhood should be abolished.

More recently, Elizabeth Ward has brought the two strands together in her book on incest, which she calls *Father-Daughter* rape. For her, the nuclear family provides the main source of such rape and also the type which illuminates many other cases. So the 'Fathers' are any trusted men — male adult relatives or family friends and the 'Daughters' are any girl children who might look to them as some kind of father figure. Once more the father is portrayed in chillingly stark terms:

> The fact that some Fathers rape Daughters means that every Daughter, theoretically, is a potential victim of rape by one of her Fathers, just as all women are potential victims of rape by any man. And the fact that girl-children are raped at home means we must question the social structure of the family. (p.94)

Are all men potential rapists? Elizabeth Ward claims that there seems to be little obvious difference between those who commit incest and those who do not. The studies so far have usually been of biological fathers, although some have also looked at step-fathers. They find that the typical incestuous father tends to be in his thirties or forties, of normal or above-average intelligence, a good worker, not involved in other criminal activities. He is often well-respected in his community and by his friends — until his incest is discovered. The typical incestuous father, she remarks, sounds like the vast majority of males in any Western country. As a clincher, Ward gives the following quote from a study of incest:

> The typical incestuous father is not mentally retarded, psychotic, or pedophilic but is characterized by some sort of personal disturbance that interferes with his ability to control his impulses in a situation where the temptation to commit incest exists. (*Meiselman*, p.108)

We are to believe, apparently, that all men have the impulse to rape young girls of their acquaintance, but that some manage to contol themselves. Furthermore, this impulse is not primarily a sexual one, but rather is an attempt to dominate, to subjugate, the daughter — and less frequently, the son. The influence of biology and upbringing both lead men to dominate women by violence, and by the creation of structures of domination in the family and through society at large. The father becomes the symbol of evil.

Fathers rape Daughters within the family; men rape women at work, in their homes, on the streets, in cars and car-parks. As long as the male principle has power to rule, at home, in the schoolyard, in the streets, at work, in culture, then we will have rape. Rape is the end result of the dehumanised authoritarian social structure called patriarchy, through which the Son becomes Father by rejecting his Mother and thereby gains unfettered access to the Daughter. (*Ward*, p.201)

The radical feminist position depends on the assumption that it is the institution of fatherhood which is responsible for the perpetuation of male dominance and exploitation within the family, and also its reflection in patriarchal control in wider forms of social organization. Given the power and anger with which the arguments are expressed it is not surprising that men, as well as women, have shown concern about the problem of fatherhood. Jeff Hearn is one of those men who wish to eliminate men's control over women's reproductive power. Not only does he want to get rid of men's sexism in all its many manifestations, but he also wants to see some rather sweeping changes made in the way we structure family life:

Most importantly, the notion of fatherhood must be smashed or more precisely dropped bit by bit into the ocean. Parenting yes, childwork yes, crèches yes, but fatherhood is the most pernicious part of the whole mess. (*Hearn*, 1983, p.51)

Jeff Hearn is not advocating that men should cease to be involved with children; on the contrary, they should become much more involved. But they need to get rid of the notions of power and property often associated with fatherhood. If they do this, not only will women be liberated from men's control, but men may also be liberated from their own dark side. Most men have very little contact with any children except their 'own' children. This might change if fatherhood as an institution were to be abolished. Perhaps then, Hearn suggests, men could develop relations of friendship and equality with children which would benefit both child and man. It is true that at the moment men are putting more investment into their own children, but does this not simply make them more inward looking? The increase in concern may be a reflection of an increased desire to 'own' their children; after all, if men are *really* concerned about children why do they give such a low priority to the provision of child care facilities?

The details of Jeff Hearn's solution seem difficult to pin down. Men are to give up control of children, but are to become much more involved in their care. I am reminded of the pithy comment from one of the mothers in a group I spoke to: "Working fathers should fill their leisure time with their children. Non-working mothers should fill their leisure time without their children." Or perhaps this from another mother: "A mother regards the children as her responsibility. A father just helps out."

Jeff Hearn worries that the more fathers become involved with their children, the more they may expect that they have rights to control them, and the mothers as well. The current concern with fatherhood may just have the effect of reinforcing patriarchal attitudes. Custody after marriage breakdown is a case in point. Just because a man has invested a certain amount of time and effort in a child does not mean that he should expect custody if his relationship with the child's mother ceases. Men have oppressed women for so long that it will take more than a few 'good' fathers to redress the balance. In particular, fatherhood has involved notions of control and authority for so long that, whatever the efforts of a few well-intentioned fathers, it is always likely to revert to its old forms.

It is hard to imagine that many men would undertake the care of children with whom they have no biological or social relationship, completely under the direction and control of the mothers of those children. In fact even if such a solution were feasible, I doubt if it would satisfy most radical feminists. Something more far-reaching would probably be required.

Feminists are divided over the question of whether differences between men and women are biologically or socially conditioned. On the whole, radical feminists are more inclined to accept that there are innate differences which cannot be eliminated by changing the way we bring up children or structure society. Given the radical feminist analysis that fatherhood is responsible for the reproduction of undesirable power structures in the family and in society as a whole, a logical conclusion for many radical feminists is that it is not worth tinkering with the father's role in order to try to improve things. The logical radical feminist conclusion seems to be the abolition of fatherhood altogether.

At first sight this might seem to be not only extreme, but also impossible. After all, we all know that men are biologically necessary — both to fertilize the egg and also because sexual reproduction confers benefits on the species. But it appears that even these certainties may rest on rather softer foundations than we realize. According to some evolutionary biologists, sexual reproduction confers few, if any, benefits to our species. If you adopt an evolutionary perspective which argues that 'the only goal of life is to reproduce itself', then it could be argued that sexual reproduction means that females waste half their reproductive potential by having to produce male children. The following hypothetical example may help to clarify this.

Suppose, among a population of creatures which reproduce sexually as we do, a mutant female occurred who could have children without needing a male to fertilize her eggs. Because only males carry the Y chromosones needed to produce male offspring all her children would be daughters — who would themselves spontaneously give birth to daughters. She, and they, would have approximately twice as many daughters as other the females in the population; and since it is usually females who look after the young, they would suffer little disadvantage in not having males around. Because of this, and their greater ability to reproduce themselves, the mutation would soon spread throughout the population and males would be eliminated. As far as females are concerned, having sons cuts down their potential for reproducing themselves.

What, then, is the point of men? Why don't human beings reproduce themselves asexually like greenfly and many other insects and plants, and abolish males altogether? The answer usually given is that sexual reproduction allows variability in a species which enables it to adapt to changes in the environment more effectively than asexual reproduction. But it appears that as far as the physical environment is concerned sex is not very useful unless the changes were much more rapid than they are now — or unless we were to have thousands more children than we do now. In any case, we human beings seem to specialize in adapting the environment to ourselves, rather than *vice versa*.

Another possible use of sexual reproduction is that it may help to protect the species against illness and disease. By mixing our genes we may make it difficult for invaders such as viruses to gain a decisive hold. But even here we are increasingly looking to technology rather than biology to protect us from illness. Jeremy Cherfas and John Gribbin have suggested that if women could discover how to reproduce without sex — make clones of themselves — they might be able to survive alone, provided they have enough high technology to keep disease at bay.

Nor is this all completely idle speculation. Parthenogenesis — the development of an egg cell without fertilization by a sperm — is quite common in some fishes and lizards, as well as in insects and plants. There have been claims that parthenogenesis can also occur in mammals, but so far there has been no decisive evidence to demonstrate this. It is however possible to get unfertilized eggs to start dividing; but the process never gets very far. There seems to be a 'missing factor' which is preventing development. If this could be found, it might one day be possible for human females to reproduce themselves without any contribution from males — and then the radical feminists' dream of a world without fathers could become a reality.

Until then the nearest approach to the abolition of fatherhood is to be found in a few self-insemination groups. Self-insemination is used by some lesbian feminists who want children, but who do not want to enter into a casual relationship with a man simply to get pregnant, and also by some heterosexual women who are concerned to maximize their reproductive freedom of choice. The male donors are often, but not always, homosexual. Sometimes they have a continuing relationship with the child; sometimes they agree to stay away and never disclose their part in the child's creation.

Nobody knows whether such fatherless families will be healthy places for a child to grow up. There are still very few of them, and since the earliest examples of self-insemination appear to have taken place in the early 1970s, it is too soon to tell what effect this environment will have on the growing child. Although many people might instinctively assume that such a family style must be harmful to a child, it may actually provide a less stressful and more secure environment than the fragment of a conventional nuclear family which is left after the fission caused by a divorce.

The lesbian family may appear to be extreme, unrelated to 'ordinary' parenthood, but I'm not so sure. In chapter one I reported that the majority of the parents I have spoken to want to minimize the differences between mothers and fathers. Furthermore, their ideal parent tended to have more 'feminine' than 'masculine' qualities. I said that what they seemed to be seeking was a 'male mother'; denying that a father has any really distinctive masculine role to play. In the lesbian family this desire seems to have come to fruition: there is one biological mother and one (occasionally more) co-mother. No doubt the co-parents find themselves playing different roles from time to time, but they are now in a position to eliminate successfully most of the major differences between motherhood and fatherhood.

The radical feminist arguments do not get much attention from the majority of parents. There is a general belief that men are not really as bad as the radical feminists make out (they probably are), and that women are not really as good as the radical feminists make out (they probably are not). Most people would completely reject the radical feminist view of the ideal parents being mother and co-mother, but the irony is that their own point of view finds its logical conclusion in just such a family structure.

There is clearly something peculiar going on. The radical feminists say that fathers are so different from mothers that they ought to be eliminated. The prevailing orthodox middle class opinion says that fathers are almost the same as mothers, which in a sense also eliminates them. Even biological science doesn't seem to be entirely sure that fathers are necessary any more.

There is much talk about involved fatherhood at present, but as we have seen there isn't quite so much action. Although there are strong pressures for fathers to participate much more in their children's lives, we live in a society which makes it hard for men to be involved in childcare, and where many children grow up without a father for much of their childhood. The question has to be asked: *is there really a need for fathers, and if so what kind of fathers do we need?*

12. The Future of Fatherhood

Modern fatherhood is in a bit of a mess. Despite the outward trappings of involvement and participation, it rests on very uncertain foundations. So much so that it has become possible to ask whether we need fathers at all. Yet despite all the criticism, I still believe in fatherhood, and I am sure that, whatever the problems, we will be able to find a style of fathering which will be right for the society in which we live, and also right for our children. This book is merely an attempt to look at the strengths and weaknesses of modern fatherhood, and to seek some ways out of the quicksands in which many fathers find themselves. There is much more to be said about fatherhood, but in this last chapter I can do no more than raise a few final issues and tentatively suggest a few directions which need further exploration.

The first point I want to make is that fatherhood is important. It means much more to men than many people suppose. To see why this is so, it is necessary to look again at motherhood. Men are jealous of motherhood; it represents a form of creativity which is always beyond us. If human life is the thing we prize most, then the creation of that life is the most important thing we can do. The tyrant may tell his victims that he has the power of life and death over them — but he lies. He has the power of death, and that is all. The power of life is far beyond him and deep down he knows it.

I sometimes wonder if all of male achievement is based on this simple fact: since men cannot create human life, they build cultures in an attempt to compensate. And then they tear them down again because the achievement is hollow. It may be too simplistic to claim that *all* male endeavour is due to this sense of impotence in the face of female creativity, but its power should never be underestimated.

Together with the jealousy, goes a sense of inferiority and inadequacy. This expresses itself in many ways, from myths which tell how men usurped women's rightful creative role, to much of the sexism and put-downs which women have to endure from men, to men's attempts to take over the act of giving birth.

Many myths, such as those of the Australian Aborigines, state quite explicitly that it was women who were the original creators of much of the natural landscape, as well as cultural inventions such as fire. But then, say the stories, men stole the women's secrets from them and now they rule instead. It has been suggested that much Aboriginal ritual and belief is based on male desire to usurp the power of women. Aboriginal boys are separated from their mothers at puberty and are circumcised. The blood of circumcision is often explicitly associated with menstrual blood or the blood of birth. In fact, some aboriginal tribes go further, and subincise their boys as well: they cut open the underside of the penis and the urethra. This operation is considered to be equivalent to turning the penis into a kind of vagina in order to try to receive the power of women. For instance, until the wound has healed, urination has to be performed in a squatting position, as women do.

Traditional Aboriginal societies were very patriarchal, and women were strictly controlled. Women often had to give birth alone, while men underwent elaborate couvade rituals and were fussed over. Bruno Bettelheim has suggested that couvade and male initiation rituals can all be explained as an acting out of male vagina envy — something which he observed in his mentally disturbed child patients. It is a tempting idea and contains more than a grain of truth, even though it can't account for all the facts.

Male envy and fear is also expressed in much male violence towards women. Pornography, as the women's movement has shown, is not primarily erotic in content, but rather attempts to subjugate the subject — usually a woman. The same impulse is expressed in rape — not always, but in the majority of cases. One of the principal themes of feminist writing is the destructiveness of men's nature and, in particular, men's hatred of women:

> *Patriarchy is itself the prevailing religion of the entire planet*, and its essential message is necrophilia. ...women are the objects of male terror, the projected personifications of "The Enemy", the real objects under attack in all the wars of patriarchy. (*Daly*, 1979, p.39)

Do men hate women? Are they really waging war against the female of the species? Not consciously perhaps, but the evidence presented by the feminists is impressive and persuasive. And the reason? It is because men are jealous and afraid of female power; a power which men cannot exercise or control. More importantly, many men do not understand the nature of women's creative power and so think that it is dangerous, like the power of death. Because they do not understand, they want to destroy or at least contain it, and the only way to do that is to destroy or control women themselves. Thus men treat women as objects; to be traded, used, defiled, reviled and degraded. The irony is that this strategy is self-deafeating. Men need the creative power of women — otherwise the species itself is doomed.

But this points the way to another possible approach. Suppose men were able to exercise creative power instead of women. Suppose that it was really men who made babies, and not women at all. Not surprisingly, this idea has cropped up time and again in different parts of the world. There are societies which claim that the mother's only part in making babies is to provide a container in which the baby can grow. All the rest is done by the father. This belief was also quite widespread in the ancient world and a classical reference may help to show its essence. In Aeschylus' *The Eumenides* Apollo defends Orestes against a charge of killing his mother by putting forward the following argument:

> This too I answer; mark a soothfast word
> Not the true parent is the woman's womb
> That bears the child; she doth but nurse the seed
> New-sown: the male is parent; she for him,
> As stranger for a stranger, hoards the germ
> Of life, unless the god its promise blight.
> And proof hereof before you I will set.
> Birth may from fathers, without mothers, be:
> See at your side a witness of the same,
> Athena, daughter of the Olympian Zeus,
> Never within the darkness of the womb
> Fostered or fashioned, but a bud more bright
> Than any goddess in her breast might bear.
> (From *Oates & O'Neill*, 1938, p.294)

Athena, the goddess of wisdom and war, was the patron of Athens. According to mythology she was born directly from the head of Zeus, wearing her full armour!

With our modern knowledge about conception and pregnancy we cannot continue to assert that the female has no part to play in the creation of a child. But there are other ways in which men can try to take over reproductive power. I have already remarked that male involvement in birth is higher in the West than in most societies throughout the world. Many writers have suggested that this is part of a male attempt to control childbirth. It is certainly possible to hear male obstetricians talking about the sense of fulfilment they feel when they deliver a baby — almost as if it were their own. This may just be the healthy identification with the patient felt by many doctors, however professionally detatched they may try to be. But it may also be a sign of attempted ownership. Ever since the invention of the forceps — a surgical instrument, and therefore the prerogative of men — men and technology have gradually become more involved in Western childbirth.

There are other, more direct, ways in which men may try to appropriate the role of women. One possibility is cloning. In the book *In His Image* David Rorvik tells the story of 'Max'. Rorvik, a science journalist, claims that in September 1973 he received a phone call from a wealthy industrialist who was prepared to spend millions of dollars in order to have a son by cloning. Rorvik's task would be to find a doctor who could solve the hundreds of intricate problems associated with such a notion. The technique is simple in theory. The nucleus would be removed from a human female egg cell and replaced with the nucleus from one of Max's cells. The egg would them be placed in a woman's womb and allowed to develop normally. Because the nucleus of the egg would only contain only Max's genes, rather than a mixture of genes from two parents as is normal, the resulting baby would be an almost exact copy of Max.

Cloning had been performed in animals, but never before in humans. The technical problems were formidable, and the ethical questions unanswered (indeed, they had hardly been asked). Nevertheless, Rorvik claims that he found a man, referred to as 'Darwin', who was prepared to undertake the task. They set up a clinic somewhere in the Third World and, with a plentiful supply of eggs from the unwitting local women — who went to the clinic for gynaecological treatment — the experiments went ahead. According to 'Darwin', "in most cases" the women knew that he was "after their eggs".

Eventually, says Rorvik, after almost one hundred implantations in four different potential host mothers they were successful, and the egg with Max's nucleus in it was carried to term by the host mother known as 'Sparrow'. She was flown to America and the baby boy was born in a small hospital in California in 1976.

When Rorvik's book appeared it caused the proverbial storm of controversy. There was even a subcommittee hearing on the subject in the House of Representatives in May 1978. The general medical concensus was that the book was a hoax, and that medical science was not yet sufficiently 'developed' to be able to clone a human. The chairman, Paul Rogers summed up by saying:

> We have learned from the scientific panel that cloning from an adult is not possible at this time. Therefore, perhaps, we are premature in thinking of ethical questions that may arise. (Quoted in *Arditti et al*, p.82)

It seems curious to suggest that we should only discuss the ethics of an act after it has been performed. Surely the right time is *before* any damage has been done. Whether or not Rorvik was recounting a true story is not important. There seems little doubt that cloning a human is theoretically possible, and that sooner or later it will be done. There is, of course, no theoretical reason why a woman should not be cloned, but one cannot help suspecting that it will be men who will be most keen to grasp the reproductive possibilities offered by the new medical techniques.

Although cloning abolishes genetic motherhood, the procedure outlined by Rorvik still requires women to bear the children. Recently, however, an even more radical possibility has been suggested. Why should men not actually become pregnant and bear children themselves? There are practical difficulties of course, but some claim that they are not necessarily insurmountable.

The most important indicator that male pregnancy might possible actually occurred in 1979, when a woman in New Zealand gave birth to a baby daughter. Nothing unusual in that, perhaps — except that the woman had had her womb removed before the start of the pregnancy! Having three daughters already, a hysterectomy was suggested as a cure for serious period problems. It appears that there must have been a fertilized egg already in her fallopian tube when the womb was removed. When the egg emerged from the tube it had no place to go. So it floated around in the abdominal cavity for a while and then implanted on the side of her intestine.

When she flew to England for a television programme, I was able to meet her. In the weeks after her hysterectomy she had actually wondered if she was pregnant, because she experienced morning sickness and a tightening in her breasts, as well as severe abdominal pain, but she just assumed that this must be an after-effect of the operation. But the symptoms persisted and she kept returning to the hospital. Not surprisingly she said nothing about her suspicion that she might be pregnant — after all, she 'knew' that it was impossible! Despite that fact that her abdomen was now quite swollen, it was not until the sixth month that one doctor was brave enough to suggest the unthinkable. An ultrasound scan soon confirmed the pregnancy, and the baby was eventually delivered by caesarian section at eight months.

The placenta was left attached to her intestine, and was gradually reabsorbed by her body. The little daughter was perfectly healthy, and when I met her she seemed to be a charming and normal seven year old. Although there have been thirty-seven other cases of pregnancy after hysterectomy, this is the only known example which has had a successful conclusion — posssibly because the fetus implanted on the most advantageous site.

Although it is still unique, this case shows clearly that a womb is not absolutely essential for the growth of a baby. Those who claim that male pregnancy is possible say that a man could be prepared by giving him female hormones, and then a fertilized egg could be implanted in a suitable site in his abdomen. The fetus would grow a placenta, just as it does in the womb and, in theory, the pregnancy could then develop normally. Delivery would have to be by caesarian section, of course, but this is now a common procedure. It is important not to underestimate the difficulties or dangers, they say, but many doctors are now confident that sometime in the 1990s some men will indeed bear children.

Other authorities are not convinced. They point out that the New Zealand woman has not felt well during the seven years since her strange pregnancy, and that she has a lot of unusual antibodies in her blood which might indicate that she was trying to reject the placenta. They also claim that the risks to both father and fetus have been seriously underestimated. The hormonal consequences, too, may be more wide-ranging than anticipated. During pregnancy, a woman produces large quantities of the female hormones, progesterone and oestrogen. If a pregnant man needed to have similar quantities in his body he would become very feminized; his facial hair would stop growing, he would develop breasts, his voice might become higher in pitch, and so on. Finally, it may be necessary to stop a pregnant man producing the male hormone, testosterone — especially if he was carrying a girl baby, because the testosterone might make the fetus become masculinized. They point out that easiest way to stop a man producing testosterone is to castrate him!

But even if the dangers and side effects could be overcome, would any man want to go through all this? The answer appears to be yes. One survey in Britain in 1986 found 60% of men against the idea of male pregnancy, 12% undecided, and 28% in favour. When the television programme I mentioned earlier placed an advertisement in the personal column of *The Guardian* newspaper asking for comments on the notion of male pregnancy, they got an enormous response. There were many men who either wanted, or were prepared, to become pregnant. Some were transsexuals, born with male genitals but with female personality traits. Some were male homosexuals who wanted children, but were unwilling or unable to find a woman to bear a child for them. To such men, the possibility of male pregnancy seems as liberating as self-insemination does to some lesbians.

Other men were prepared to consider it because of infertility. If this was the only way for the couple to have a child then, as a last resort, the man would be prepared to carry the child instead of his wife. Finally, there were some men who simply liked the idea of being pregnant and giving birth to a child. One man I spoke to was very matter-of-fact about this. Since he has been a child he had wanted to have a baby, and at last there was the possibility of turning his fantasy into fact. He is married with two children, and not at all fanatical in his desire. I doubt very much if he would would actually take steps to become pregnant, even if the opportunity were offered to him.

There are two aspects to the possibilities opened up by modern medical science. In practical terms they do offer the chance for men to take even more control over reproduction, and further dominate women. There is an urgent need for a widespread public debate about all of the issues raised by fertility control, genetic counselling, testing for fetal 'abnormalities', and so on. The possibility of the extension of oppressive patriarchy must also be considered in this debate.

But the new technologies also offer us new ways of thinking. They help to broaden the debate about fatherhood even further. I have already remarked that today many couples discuss what their working arrangements will be after the birth of the baby. Most of them still end up doing the traditional thing, but the very fact that the discussion has taken place is indicative of a new attitude towards parental roles. Similarly it will become theoretically possible for a couple to say, 'Right, we agree that we want to have a baby. Now, which one of us is going to get pregnant?' Of course, in practice, women will continue to have babies because it is safer, cheaper, and more natural for them to do so. But the fact that the question could have been asked has broadened the agenda of parenthood, and may be instrumental in changing male attitudes towards pregnancy and birth.

I hope that this will help to heal some of the wounds which have opened up between the sexes. Certainly, at the moment childbirth is a very sensitive issue for many women. The responses of the women who were asked about male pregnancy were nearly all expressed in political terms. Those who were against it said that men shouldn't bear children because they don't even take a proper share in their upbringing when they're born. Those who were in favour said that it would be a good thing for men to get pregnant, because it would serve them right and show them just what women have to put up with! There is a need for reconciliation between mothers and fathers, and this cannot come about unless both will recognize the importance of the other's role.

The desire to father is deep, complex, and flawed. It is also very powerful. It should now be clear that the chance of abolishing fatherhood, as the radical feminists would like, is very small indeed. For better or worse, men will continue to insist on playing a part in the making and bringing up of children. Furthermore, I believe that it is naive to assume that getting rid of the father will really benefit the mother or child.

The radical feminist critique of male oppression is telling and accurate. But the conclusions they reach are incomplete, and ultimately misleading. The problem with radical feminism is that it often becomes a closed system. As a brief example, consider the question of violence. Male violence against wives and children is a key part of the feminist evidence. Yet there are women who injure their children, and wives who batter their husbands. If one were to be true to the radical feminist analysis, one would have to agree that woman's nature, too, is corrupt. But it has become an article of faith for some women that all evil springs from the male of the species, and so female violence is attributed to the corrupting influence of patriarchy rather than any dark side of femininity. It is the same with every other objection. It is impossible to refute the radical feminist picture of the world because it is based on female fear and jealousy of men — the mirror image of the male jealousy and fear which it has so dramatically exposed.

There is, furthermore, a vast quantity of evidence which suggests that fathers do have a positive part to play in the nurture and upbringing of children — although a note of caution is necessary because much of the research relies on comparing fatherless families with those where the father is present. Such comparisons are not always valid, because the fatherless families tend to be poorer, to have worse social conditions such as housing or education, and may well suffer more family strain and disruption. Any differences between the two types of family may be due to these social factors, rather than to any direct influence from the presence or absence of a father.

Nevertheless the sheer volume of evidence seems enough to indicate that some very positive benefits flow when children are able to enjoy a close, stable and loving relationship with a father. Researchers have found a relationship between father-absence and many personality problems including juvenile delinquency, poor academic achievement, inability to adjust to stress, inadequate development of conscience (for boys only, girls seem unaffected), and difficulty in adjusting to appropriate sex roles.

The effect of the father in the development of sex role behaviour in both boys and girls has been studied in some detail, mainly by American researchers. It appears that both boys and girls are more secure in their relationships with the opposite sex and with their own peers if there was a good relationship with the father. Homosexual men and women are more likely to have had a poor relationship with the father than heterosexuals. Both men and women with stable marriages are likely to describe their relationship with the father as satisfactory. One study (*Fisher*) went so far as to suggest that women with a poor father relationship have fewer orgasms than women with a good father relationship!

One example of the sort of work that has been done is the study carried out by E.M. Hetherington, who compared three matched groups of lower middle-class girls (13-17 yrs) who regularly attended a community recreation centre. There were girls whose fathers were absent because of divorce, and had had no contact since; girls whose fathers had died; and girls with both parents living. None of the girls had a brother, all were first children and none had adult males living in house (except the third group,of course). Both groups of father-absent girls had great difficulty in interacting comfortably with men and males of their own age, although all the girls were comortable with other girls and with adult women. Daughters of widows tended to be very shy and sat as far away from male interviewers as possible. They exhibited avoidance behaviour; often sitting stiffly upright, leaning backwards, keeping legs together and avoiding eye contact. Girls whose father had left because of divorce tended to sit as close as possible to the interviewers (girls from two-parent families sat at an intermediate range) and to sprawl in their chairs, have open leg posture, lean slightly forward and exhibit much eye contact and smiling. Other studies have also suggested that father-absent girls are sexually more knowledgeable and precocious.

It has also been claimed that boys exhibit 'low masculinity' if fathers are also not very masculine — especially if the mother dominates at home. If dad has a high level of decision making in the family, the son will tend to be more masculine. The child's perception of his father's dominance at home seems to be more important than the amount of dominance behaviour that the father actually displays. But there are limits to this effect. If a dominant father consistently puts down his son, then the boy will not be able to develop his masculinity so easily. In fact, masculine development seems to be best served when the father is both masculine and also has a warm and loving relationship with his child.

There also appears to be a link between the 'dominance' of the father in family life and the way boys adjust to adolescence and adulthood. This tends to be easier if the father was the 'dominant' parent. Even when fathers are present in the families of delinquent boys, they tend to be weak, and to defer to the mother in the majority of decisions. Some studies report the same findings for girls, while others suggest that girls develop best when each parent is positively involved in family decision making. Both boys and girls from 'mother-dominated' families appear to find it harder to make stable relationships.

Many of these studies are open to question. Their assumptions about 'masculinity' and 'femininity' are not always clear, for instance. What they do suggest most strongly though, is that there is a need for fathers. Although bad fathers may do great harm to their children, good fathers can be most helpful. On balance, the evidence seems to suggest that it better for the emotional and mental health of a child to be brought up by a father as well as a mother, because he has something different and vital to offer his offspring. But there is a need for caution. Just as some biologists may overestimate the influence of genes and hormones on a child's personality, so some psychologists overestimate the effect of upbringing. Fathers are important, but they do not determine absolutely their children's development. Between the twin limitations of nature and nurture there is still room for free will and personal choice. I recently came across a most charming expression of this in a seventeenth century commentary on the genealogy of Jesus:

> Rehoboam begat Abiam: a bad father begat a bad son. Abiam begat Asa: a bad father a good son. Asa begat Jehoshaphat: a good father a good son. Jehoshaphat begat Joram: a good father a bad son. I see, Lord, from hence, that my father's piety cannot be entailed; that is bad news for me. But I see also that actual impiety is not always

hereditary; that is good news for my son. (Thomas Fuller, *Scripture Observations*, 1645. Quoted in *Hastings*, 1963.)

Another conclusion seems to come from all this research: not only does a child need a father as well as a mother, but each has a different role to play. This goes against both radical feminist and prevailing liberal middle class ideas, as we saw in the last chapter. I am not in favour of the extreme, almost caricatured, stereotypes of mother and father which have sometimes been peddled, but I am now convinced that unisex parenthood is not a good idea. The modern tendency to deny gender differences is based partly on a desire to escape the oppression of constricting and controlling role models, but also because it means that we do not have to make evaluations which might have moral dimension attached. Not only is it a cop-out, it doesn't work.

If there is to be a difference between mothers and fathers, where shall we seek its proper manifestation? The key is perhaps to be found in the relative detachment of the father. No matter how involved the father is in the birth of his children, there is always a sense in which he is more distant from the baby than the mother. This sense of separation may be profoundly distressing to the new father, and he may strive to get as close as possible to his newborn — even going to the extent of trying to take over the processes of birth and feeding and nurturing. Yet there is value, both for the child and for the family as a whole, in the father's detachment. For if the mother is very close to the child, so is the child close to the mother. But this is a situation which must not last if the child is to grow and mature into an independent adult. The committed father has a very important part to play in this process of separation and maturing. "From the moment of birth the child grows towards the father" as Margaret Mead put it.

The father represents separation and individuality, just as the mother represents incorporation and communality. Both are important in life, and the child which experiences both as positive and loving experiences is well set on the road to maturity. It would be a tragedy if mothers and fathers were never to reverse these roles - for the father to enfold, and the mother to draw out — but in most families this will represent the basic pattern for the majority of the time.

But it must be recognized that for many committed fathers this seems to be a hard and unrewarding role to play. It appears to imply harshness, lack of feeling, and an emphasis on the outside world which conflicts with loyalty to the family. In times past this has often been the case. A sense of alienation from the family is part of men's general malaise at being unable

to create in the way that women can. Yet we cannot escape from it, even with the possibility of male pregnancy, and it has to be accepted.

What we need is a new definition of fatherhood: one that will build on the strengths of our present freedom and fluidity, but which will be both realistic and inspirational in the model it presents to fathers. It will not be easy, and it will take time. Mostly it will come about through hard, and sometimes bitter, experience. It will draw on new insights about the differences between men and women, and in particular, explorations of the limits of variability. We know that there are cultures in which men are expected to be nurturing and gentle, and other cultures where they are expected to be aggressive and distant from their children. We cannot divorce our ideas of fatherhood from our ideas about the kind of society we want. Nevertheless, there is not an infinite scope for flexibility. There *are* innate differences between men and women, and that means also between mothers and fathers.

It is obvious that we need to continue to press for changes in the practical arrangement of society if committed fatherhood is to become a reality. But even more importantly we need to rethink some of our prejudices and presuppositions, and in the space left to me I just want to look at two areas where I think there needs to be a major shift in attitude from both men and women if we are to construct a new model of fatherhood which can draw on some of the gains we have made recently, while also eliminating some of the weaknesses of our present position.

It is possible to get the measure of an age by looking at the prevailing attitudes towards pairs of linked concepts. Two of these are *freedom* and *equality*, and *rights* and *duties*. Such terms tend to be used as slogans, especially by those who are comfortable in entrenched political positions. The Right is fond of talking about 'freedom', while the Left prefers to seek 'equality'. Similarly, 'duties' are espoused by the Right, while 'rights' are found on the Left! A full exploration of these concepts offers a very fruitful way of exploring political and moral theories. For instance, is it possible to have both freedom and equality, or is it always necessary to come to some sort of compromise? Are rights and duties just opposite sides of the same coin, or do they express fundamentally different ethical positions?

Yet most of us use these concepts, and think in terms of the oppositions they provide, without ever really analysing them. Rather, they act like symbols for us, containing a package of half-formed ideas, opinions and feelings. Most of the time this causes no problem, but instead helps us to make quick judgements without having to start from first principles each time. But occasionally, they get in the way of a clearer view of the world, and then it is time to look at them more critically.

The notion of *duty* is one such concept, which needs to be looked at again in the context of fatherhood. There is now a widespread, though implicit, assumption that fathers have no real duties towards their children. In fact, I would argue that much of modern feminist thinking is based on this assumption, and that it needs to be challenged. I think that as men begin to get more involved as fathers they will start to recognize again that it entails responsibilities which are more far-reaching than almost any other human endeavour, and that as this happens they will also view their rights and duties in a radically new way.

The active father wants equality with his partner. He will share care and share work if appropriate; he will look after the children full time if appropriate; he will work full time if appropriate. But however much time he manages to spend with his children — and it will be a lot — he will want to share responsibility. He will not leave all the decisions to his partner because he is too lazy or too insecure to make them himself. Nor will he be happy if she wants to make all the domestic decisions herself, because she feels threatened by him, or because she sees it as part of her role as a mother.

Increasingly, the father will view his relationship with the children as a thing in its own right, separate from, though complementary to, his partner's. The very fact of his paternity — however defined — will be sufficient for him to feel that he has certain rights and duties with respect to the child. One particularly complex and controversial area where this may find expression concerns abortion politics. The committed father may come to feel increasingly unhappy about the notion of 'a woman's right to choose' an abortion. He will argue that a child is a joint responsibility and a joint charge. Whatever his views on the morality of abortion itself, he will argue that it should not be allowed unless *both* parents are happy for it to be performed. The fact that a woman carries the greater burden through her nine months of pregnancy is an accident of nature, not of will. It is not sufficient to give her greater rights over the unborn child than those of the father. Of course, if she did not want the child but he did, then it would be incumbent upon *him* to provide for the child and bring it up after it is born.

Many people argue that men's indifference to paternity is the justification for women having the final say in abortion choice. A man can always run away from the child, a woman cannot. Therefore the woman must make the choice. Of course, a woman can also run away from her child after it has been born, but the double standard applies: a man who deserts his children is considered less of a sinner than the woman who does the same. The active father despises the double standard. He does not consider the man less guilty — in fact he is likely to judge him more harshly. Giving women the final say in abortion, though, only reinforces the double standard — it allows the man to walk out without having to worry about the consequences of his actions.

Abortion is an emotive and difficult area. It affects all of us directly or indirectly, and our attitudes to it are constantly subject to change. For some years it has been seen as a way of liberating women; of allowing them to be as free from the restrictions of biology as men are. We may come to revise that position. The active father would certainly say that men's freedom from biology is illusory, and that a lack of committment is not freedom but loss. For him, the birth of a child is not the end of life, but the beginning; not the end of a care-free existence, but the start of caring; not the end of freedom, but the start of liberation.

The abortion debate has nearly always been framed in terms of the concept of *rights*. Although it is inevitable that this should be so, there are some dangerous side effects — side effects which might also come from a greater paternal involvement in childcare. The risk is that we get a greater emphasis on the possession or ownership of children. Both men and women are liable to fall into this trap — Adrienne Rich's caustic definition of fatherhood in the previous chapter spoke of the father as a male who has possession of a female and *her* offspring. Although she would probably deny that she meant that a child *belongs* to its mother as a slave belongs to its master, it is hard to be completely free from such notions as long as we continue to use the language of possession. Shulamith Firestone, one of the most radical of feminists, claims that only artificial reproduction can free women from feelings of ownership. The phrase, used by many women, 'just think what I went through to have you' is a recipe for thinking that the child 'belongs' to the mother, she says.

Kahlil Gibran makes the same point more beautifully in *The Prophet*:

> Your children are not your children.
> They are the sons and daughters of Life's longing for itself.
> They come through you but not from you,
> And though they are with you yet they belong not to you.

If we start to think of the *duties* which fathers (and mothers) have towards their children, we will be less likely to treat children as possessions. The notion of duty is unpopular today, and service is almost a dirty word. It is considered demeaning to the freedom of the individual to suggest that one person should serve another. Yet parenthood requires selflessness, and the questions of duty and service will come up again, in an acute form, when considering the question of authority in the family.

Indeed, I think that the notion of authority may be the single most important challenge facing fatherhood today - and perhaps even society at large. Of all the values associated with the traditional father it is his authority which has been challenged most strongly and discredited most thoroughly. Yet I have now come to believe that it is vital to re-examine the idea, and see whether it is possible to redefine it so that the role of the father may have a positive contribution to make to the dynamics of the family.

I am not referring to the kind of vulgar right-wing sloganizing which exorts us to "Put Dad back at the head of the table" as a spokesman for the 'Conservative Family Campaign' recently put it. This kind of call has been going on for years; in the 1950s a book on fatherhood informed us that:

> Plainly this nation needs father in the armchair at the head of the table again, carving the roast, disciplining the children, keeping the peace, settling the disputes, loving his wife but reserving his pants for his own use, serving as an example for sons to emulate and daughters to seek in husbands of their own. (*English & Foster*, p.xiii)

This seems closer to authoritarianism than the kind of authority that I am looking for. The urgent need in the family is to find a way of expressing authority without domination, power-seeking, or oppression. I suspect that the only way such authority can be found or exercised is by adopting the way of the servant. If a man or woman wishes to have authority in the household then they must serve the other members; not because they are coerced or maneuvered into it, but freely and with dignity. Authority, conceived in these terms, is not a relationship to a subordinate carried out by force of arms or influence of hormones. Rather it is a quality of personhood which is exercised by giving to others, just as Jesus washed his disciples' feet, rather than they his. Looked at in these terms, any attempt to dominate others will automatically result in a loss of authority rather than an increase.

Such ideas need a lot of working through, but they seem to me to offer the possibility of a positive answer to the problem of the uncertain father. If men are to discover a new sense of purpose in their parenthood then we must either return to the patriarchal family structure of the Victorians or else try to create new relationships with a different basis.

I wrote this book because I wanted to try to understand some of the paradoxes of modern fatherhood. It has been a fascinating journey, and some of the conclusions and discoveries have surprised me. In the course of the book I have become ever more aware of the dilemma of the modern father: his reasons for wanting to be a father, his uncertainty about his paternity, the pressures that force him towards power sharing and involvement; the rituals which help him to find confidence in his new status and role; the social conditions which ultimately betray him and prevent the achievement of his ideal; and the questioners who wonder whether it would be better if we abolished fathers altogether. Indeed, there were times when I felt like calling it, *The Tragedy of the Modern Father*. But it has thrown up many fruitful ideas for me, and my own exploration will continue, with a closer look at some of the ideas presented in this last chapter.

I have not lost my faith in fatherhood, nor am I despondent about the future. Families need fathers and men need fatherhood. There may be sorrows, but they are outweighed by the joys; there may be uncertainty, but it is overwhelmed by the satisfactions; there may be a lack of physical creativity, but helping to raise children remains the most creative work most of us will ever attempt; there may be pain at the recognition of men's will to power, but there is opportunity for self-discovery and redemption. The relationships we make with our children are amongst the most intense and precious that we will ever know. The present state of fatherhood may be uncertain, but its future is assured.

Notes

[1] The example of the Old Testament prophets comes from *Salzman*. For an example of a society in Burma which swings between two completely different kinds of political organization, see Leach 1954. He describes the Kachin tribes as oscillating between democratic and autocratic extremes. In practice, most tribes operate a kind of compromise system which varies in its distance from the two extremes according to local circumstances.

[2] The Mormon studies were conducted by Victor Christopherson and are reported in *Benson*, 1968, p.144.

[3] For John Bowlby, the psychologist who invented the term *maternal deprivation*, the father was of very little direct importance to the child:

> In the young child's eyes father plays second fiddle and his value increases only as the child becomes more able to stand alone. Nevertheless, as the illegitimate child knows, fathers have their uses even in infancy. Not only do they provide for their wives to enable them to devote themselves unrestrictedly to the care of infant and toddler, but, by providing love and companionship, they support the mother emotionally and help her maintain that harmonious contented mood in the atmosphere of which her infant thrives. (p.15)

[4] The quotation is from The *First Years of Life*, to be published by the Community Education Department of the Open University in 1987.

[5] In the US in 1984, 51.8% of married women with children under six were in some kind of employment. (In 1960 the comparable figure was only 18.6%).

Source: *Statistical Abstract of the United States 1985*. Washington DC: Bureau of the Census 1984.

In the UK in 1983 24% of women whose youngest child was in the age range 0-4 were in some kind of employment (18% part time, 5% full time). The comparable figure for women with no dependent children was 65% (46% full time, 18% part time).

Source: *General Household Survey 1983*. Office of Population Censuses and Surveys. London: Her Majesty's Stationery Office 1985.

[6] The Rebelsky & Hanks study has been sometimes cited by writers in order to show how uninvolved fathers really are. But before throwing up our hands in despair it is worth noting that other researchers have pointed out that vocalization may not be a particularly good indicator of a father's involvement with such young children (mothers seem to talk more to their children). Also, there were only ten fathers in the sample so it is dangerous to draw wide-ranging conclusions.

Other studies have come up with less spectacular findings. For instance, Frank Pederson and Kenneth Robson, using mothers' accounts, found that fathers spent between forty-five minutes and twenty-six hours a week playing with their nine-month-old children.

Charlie Lewis found that only 4% of the fathers in his sample played with their one-year-olds less than ten minutes a day. Two-thirds spent between thirty minutes and two hours a day, and 12% spent more than two hours a day playing with their children. (1986, p.119)

[7] See *Bloch* for the notion that kinship ties provide the basis for a morality of long-term reciprocity.

[8] Ideas about the purpose of marriage also seem to be in a state of flux at present. In the *Book of Common Prayer* the following reasons for marriage are given:

> First, It was ordained for the procreation of children, ... Secondly, It was ordained for a remedy against sin, and to avoid fornication; ... Thirdly, It was ordained for the mutual society, help, and comfort, that the one ought to have of the other...

In the 1960s and 70s a wave of new services and approaches to marriage appeared. The Church of England's *Alternative Service Book* is a typical example. It effectively reverses the order of the old Prayer Book's three reasons for marriage:

> Marriage is given that husband and wife may comfort and help each other, ... It is given, that with delight and tenderness they may know each other in love, ... It is given, that they may have children and be blessed in caring for them...

For the liturgical reformers, marriage was no longer to be thought of as primarily for the procreation of children. But I wonder whether those outside the Church agree. Increasingly, young couples seem to live together for companionship and physical fulfillment, and only take the step of getting married when they want to have children. Perhaps marriage is all about having babies after all.

[9] The word *couvade* was coined by Sir Edward Tylor from the French verb *couver*, meaning 'to brood'. Anthropologists use the term to describe ritual processes, while psychologists use it to describe psychological or psychosomatic symptoms. I am not convinced that there is any point in maintaining such a distinction. As far as I am concerned, couvade symptoms in the West play the same role as couvade rituals in other cultures. They have a ritual function, but are merely expressed in the individualistic idiom which we commonly adopt, rather than in the more collective style characteristic of many traditional societies.

Although some so-called couvade symptoms are clearly pathological, I do not accept that this applies to most of them. As we will see in chapter six, couvade is a perfectly natural phenomenon, given the prevailing social circumstances in the West.

[10] The quotes from Andy, John, Ian, Stuart and Chris in this and other chapters are taken from a group discussion I led for two Open University courses on pregnancy and birth (1985a & b). Many of them are included in the edited highlights provided on audio cassette with the published courses.

[11] Several studies show the dramatic nature of the change which has swept through our society in only twenty years. For instance, in the United States in 1972 only 27% of fathers were present at birth. It was not until 1974 that the American College of Obstetricians and Gynaecologists endorsed the father's presence. But by 1980 about 80% of fathers attended (Parke).

A similar pattern can be found in Britain. Between 1950 and 1970 fathers were only present at 15% of deliveries. After 1970 the figure rose to 70% and some studies have shown figures as high as 92% in the 1980s (*Woollett et al*). In Australia only 0.7% of men attended delivery in 1962, but by the 1980s this had increased to nearly 80% (Russell).

[12] Anne Woollett asked women who had given birth between the 1940s and the 1970s whether they had wanted their husbands to be present at birth, and also whether the men actually were there. Her figures show the lag between women's wishes and men's compliance:

Fathers at Birth	**1940s**	**1950s**	**1960s**	**1970s**
Mother wanted father to be present:	14.3%	38.9%	50.0%	73.1%
Father was present	none	8.5%	32.2%	64.0%

Figures presented at a meeting of the Fatherhood Research Group on 3rd July 1985.

[13] A review of the evidence on the effects of fathers at birth can be found in *Woollett et al*, pp.74ff.

[14] The West London Hospital survey is reported in *Brant*, p.125. The responses were as follows:

Helped to sustain morale	615
Provided physical comfort	147
Helped with breathing	112
Furthered husband/wife relationship	56
Wife appreciated sharing experience	23
Helped pass instructions	11
Eased pain	10

About a third of the men (251) identified some aspect of the labour which they found upsetting.

Wife's pain	116
Helplessness	25
Attitude of staff and lack of attention	24
Blood and placenta	18
Forceps	9
Emergence of head	9

[15] Although these beliefs were held until recently, the present position is less clear. Now that native peoples have been exposed to missionaries, explorers, and others with Western knowledge and beliefs, it is harder to distinguish between their ideas and ours. There has also been controversy about the exact nature of these beliefs. Some anthropologists maintain that the people 'really' know that there is a connection between intercourse and conception, but they choose to deny it because it fits in with their social system. Other anthropologists say that there is 'real' ignorance, but point out that we should not confuse ignorance with stupidity and thereby claim that such people are 'primitive' or 'savage'. Details of this so-called 'virgin birth' debate can be found in *Leach*, 1969, *Barnes*, 1973, and volumes 3, 4, 6, 7 & 10 of *Man* - the journal of the Royal Anthropological Institute.

[16] The study of reactions to father/child resemblances is reported in *Daly & Wilson*.

[17] Most AID practitioners try to get round the problem of legal paternity by telling their clients to continue making love during the treatment, and in particular on those days when the woman is artificially inseminated. This is supposed to make the biological paternity uncertain and keep open the possibility that the husband is the biological father. This is generally quite unrealistsic since the whole reason for AID is usually the known infertility of the husband.

[18] While there is no doubt that some parents do feel a kind of rapturous kinship with their new born, it is misleading to assert that this is necessary to the development of good parenting. The research is ambiguous in this respect.

A study by *Richards et al* found a relationship between father's birth attendance and his level of involvement with the child at 30 weeks, but not at 60 weeks. They suggest that this is because fathers who wanted to be present at birth were also likely to get involved in childcare. *Peterson et al* found a similar sort of link, and suggest the father's experience of labour and birth is more important than his attitudes before birth in determining his subsequent involvement.

Participation, rather than simple attendance, seems to be the key in two studies (reported in *Beail*, p.12) which suggest that fathers who were excluded from birth because a ceasarian section was performed were more involved than other fathers. It has been suggested that the reason for this is their greater involvement after birth while the mother was recovering from the section.

Other studies have found no significant link between father participation at birth and future involvement (*Woollett et al*) and it is clear that much more work needs to be done - especially on trying to get some agreement about the meaning of terms such as 'involvement' and 'participation'.

[19] It may seem obvious that the primary aim of obstetrics should be the delivery of a healthy child, but if this is achieved at the price of damaging the mother or father's ability to parent then the price may be too high. If bad socialization at the time of birth had a part to play in subsequent malpractice such as baby battering, then it might be better to pay a little less attention to the baby, and a bit more to the parents. There is no perfect recipe for success, but at present, because his work is finished when the baby is born, the obstetrician has little incentive to look beyond birth to the wider aspects of parenting.

[20] For more on the ritual of birth see *Kitzinger*, 1978, *Seel*, 1986, and *Davis-Floyd*. For

more on hi-tech childbirth and postnatal depression see *Welburn* and *Oakley*. For the hormonal theory, see *Dalton*.

[21] Incidentally, this particular episode illustrates one of the great advantages of fathers' groups. If a group of men get together, to relax and talk about fathering there is a wonderful opportunity for any worries such as David's to be expressed. All he needed to know was that his response was 'normal'. But if he hadn't come to the meeting he might never have been in a position to raise the matter with another father.

Some men are able to talk to colleagues at work, others are not so lucky. One man I met, a merchant banker, had no-one at work to whom he could talk, except the senior partner who had just become a grandfather. None of the other young executives were prepared to discuss domestic matters; perhaps because they thought it might show weakness in such a highly competitive environment. On the other hand, another new father displayed obvious relish when recounting how the only woman in his office was being instructed and supported during her first pregnancy by her three colleagues, all young fathers keen to share their greater experience.

[22] In a letter to *Pediatrics*, 1972, Derrick & Patrice Jelliffe (authors of a standard textbook on breastfeeding) write on induced lactation. They note that, "lactation induced by sucking stimulation is reported in adult men, a surprising finding perhaps, until one pauses to reflect that milk production is well recognized in males in the form of neonatal Hexenmilch" The reference they give for this is Gates, Helen, 1972, 'Abnormal Lactation' (in press) - which I have not been able to track down any further. (Hexenmilch, 'witch's milk' is a milk-like secretion produced from the nipples of some new born babies, both male and female.)

[23] There is some evidence to suggest that lactating women are less interested in sex than bottle feeding women - probably for hormonal reasons. A study by Alder and Bancroft of 25 women found that none of the six bottle feeders had any loss of interest in sex, while all the lactating women reported a reduction of interest. They also found that the breastfeeding women had lower levels of circulating androgens, male hormones often felt to have a role in the level of libido. The sample in this study is small but the findings agree with the anecdotal evidence which I have come across.

[24] Several countries in the EEC already have some form of parental leave and the Community proposals are, in part, designed to harmonize the different provisions. There are a lot of variations and special conditions, but the following table gives a broad indication of the position in 1985.

Country	Length of leave	Who entitled	Pay
Belgium	3 months, up to 4 years extension	Public employees	Unpaid
Denmark	10 weeks	All	90%
France	2 years	All in public sector; only women in private	Unpaid
Greece	3 months	Private sector	Unpaid
Ireland	NONE		
Italy	6 months	All	30%
Luxembourg	1 year	Public sector	Unpaid
Netherlands	NONE		

Portugal	6 months/2 years	All	Unpaid
Spain	NONE		
UK	NONE		
West Germany	3 years	Public sector	Unpaid

Source: *House of Lords*

[25] *House of Lords*. p.195. Many men I know will take time off work to look after a sick child, but they will usually have to lie about it and pretend that they were themselves ill. It's not a very satisfactory system.

[26] A register of job sharing opportunities around London is kept by New Ways To Work, 309 Upper Street, London N1 2TY [01-226 0246]. They also have details of similar organizations in other parts of the UK.

[27] This is a course produced by the Community Education Department of the Open University. It is designed to help parents adjust to life with a new baby or toddler. It is due to be published by the Open University Press in January 1977.

[28] Of the 54 women I asked, 17 (31%) thought housework more important to motherhood than fatherhood, 28 (52%) thought it equally important to each, and 9 (17%) thought it more important to fatherhood. I only managed to ask eight men this question; five thought housework equally important for mothers and fathers, while the other three thought it more important to motherhood.

[29] The research with rats is reported in *Quadnago & Rockwell* and in *Goldberg. Money & Tucker* (pp.68-71) describe the case of the boy who was reassigned as a girl. This is commented on in *Durden-Smith & de Simone* (p.90ff), who also describe the Dominican Republic gender changes (p.87ff).

References and Bibliography

Alder, E. & Bancroft, J. "Sexual behaviour of lactating women" in *Reproductive and Infant Psychology* 1983 **1**:47-52.

Alder, E., Cook, A., Davidson, D., West, C., & Bancroft, J. "Hormones, mood and sexuality in lactating women" in *British Journal of Psychiatry* 1986 **184**:74-79.

Appleton, William. *Fathers and Daughters*. New York: Doubleday 1981, London: Papermac 1982.

Arditti, Rita; Klein, Renate & Minden, Shelley. *Test-Tube Women: What Future for Motherhood?* London & Boston: Pandora Press 1984.

Balaskas, Janet. *The Active Birth Partners Handbook*. London: Sidgwick & Jackson 1984.

Barber, Dulan. *Unmarried Fathers*. London: Hutchinson 1975.

Barnes, John. "Genetrix:Genitor::Nature:Culture?" in Goody (ed) 1973.

Beail, Nigel. "Role of the father during pregnancy and birth" in Beail & McGuire (eds) 1982.

Beail, Nigel & McGuire, Jacqueline (eds). *Fathers: Psychological Perspectives*. London: Junction Books 1982.

Bell, Colin; McKee, Lorna & Priestley, Karen. *Fathers, Childbirth and Work*. Manchester: Equal Opportunities Commission, Quay Street, M3 3HN, 1983.

Benson, Leonard. *Fatherhood: a Sociological Perspective*. New York: Random House 1968.

Bettelheim, Bruno. *Symbolic Wounds*. London: Thames & Hudson 1955.

Biller, Henry. *Father, Child, and Sex Role*. Lexington: D.C. Heath 1971.

Biller, Henry & Meredith, Dennis. *Father Power*. New York: David McKay 1974.

Bloch, Maurice. "The long term and the short term: the economic and political significance of the morality of kinship" in Goody (ed) 1973.

Bott, Elizabeth. *Family and Social Network*. London: Tavistock Publications 1971.

Bradley, Robert. *Husband-Coached Childbirth*. New York: Harper & Row 1965. (Third edition 1981)

Brain, Robert. *Bangwa Kinship and Marriage*. Cambridge: University Press 1972.

Brain, Robert. *Friends and Lovers*. London: Hart-Davis, MacGibbon 1976

Brant, Herbert. *Childbirth for Men*. Oxford: University Press 1985.

Brownmiller, Susan. *Against Our Will: Men, Women and Rape*. New York: Simon & Schuster, London: Martin Secker & Warburg 1975.

Cammarata, Jerry & Leighton, Frances Spatz. *The Fun Book of Fatherhood*. Los Angeles: Pinnacle Books 1979.

Cherfas, Jeremy & Gribbin, John. *The Redundant Male*. London: Paladin 1985.

Chesler, Phyllis. *About Men*. London: The Women's Press. New York: Simon & Schuster 1978.

Conn, Charles. *FatherCare: What it Means to be God's Child*. Waco, Texas: Word Incorporated 1983. London: Word Publishing 1985.

Dalton, Katherina. *Depression After Childbirth*. Oxford: University Press 1980.

Daly, Martin & Wilson, Margo. "Whom are newborn babies said to resemble?" in *Ethnology and Sociobiology* 1982 **3**:69-78.

Daly, Mary. *Beyond God the Father: Toward a Philosophy of Women's Liberation*. Boston: Beacon Press 1973.

Daly, Mary. *Gyn/Ecology: The Metaethics of Radical Feminism*. Boston: Beacon Press 1978. London: The Women's Press 1979.

Davies, Hunter. *Father's Day: Scenes from Domestic Life*. London: Weidenfeld & Nicholson 1981.

Davis-Floyd, Robbie. "Birth as an American rite of passage" in Michaelson (ed) 1986.

Dawkins, Richard. *The Selfish Gene*. Oxford: University Press 1976.

Dawson, Warren. *The Custom of Couvade*. Manchester: University Press 1929.

Diagram Group. *Dad's Baby*. London: Corgi Books 1986.

Dick-Read, Grantly. *Childbirth Without Fear: The Principles and Practice of Natural Childbirth*. London: William Heinemann 1942.

Douglas, Mary. "Couvade and menstruation" in *Implicit Meanings*. Boston and London: Routledge & Kegan Paul 1975.

Durden-Smith, Jo & de Simone, Diane. *Sex and the Brain*. London: Pan 1983.

Ehrenreich, Barbara. *The Hearts of Men: American Dreams and the Flight from Commitment*. New York: Anchor Press/Doubleday, London: Pluto Press 1983.

Eisenstein, Hester. *Contemporary Feminist Thought*. Boston: G.K.Hall, London & Sydney: Unwin Paperbacks 1984.

English, Spurgeon & Foster, Constance. *Fathers Are Parents, Too*. London: George Allen & Unwin 1953.

Enoch, M. David & Trethowan, W.H. *Uncommon Psychiatric Syndromes*. Bristol: John Wright 1979.

Evans, Ruth & Durward, Lyn. *Maternity Rights Handbook*. London: Penguin 1984.

Evans-Pritchard, Edward. *The Nuer*. Oxford: The Clarendon Press 1940.

Evans-Pritchard, Edward. *Kinship and Marriage among the Nuer*. Oxford: The Clarendon Press 1951.

Fein, Robert. "Research on fathering: social policy and an emergent perspective" in the *Journal of Social Issues* 1978 **34**:122-35.

Fenwick, Peter & Elizabeth. *The Baby Book for Fathers*. London: Angus & Robertson 1978.

Finch, John. "Paternalism and professionalism in childbirth" in the *New Law Journal* 21st & 28th October 1982.

Firestone, Shulamith. *The Dialectic of Sex: The Case for Feminist Revolution*. London: Jonathan Cape 1970.

Fisher, S.F. *The Female Orgasm: Psychology, Physiology, Fantasy*. New York: Basic Books 1973.

Francis, Martin. *Fathering for Men*. Bristol: Generation Books 1986.

Genné, William. *Husbands, Wives and Pregnancy*. New York: Association Press 1956. London: Darwen Finlayson 1957.

Gennep, Arnold van. *The Rites of Passage*. (English translation by Monika Vizedom & Gabrielle Caffee). London: Routledge & Kegan Paul 1960.

Gibran, Kahlil. *The Prophet*. London: Heinemann 1926.

Goldberg, Steven. *The Inevitability of Patriarchy*. London: Temple Smith 1977. (This is an extensive revision of the American edition first published in 1973.)

Goody, Jack (ed). *The Character of Kinship*. Cambridge: University Press 1973.

Green, Maureen. *Goodbye Father*. London: Routledge & Kegan Paul 1976. (Published in US as *Fathering*. New York: McGraw-Hill 1976.)

Greenberg, Martin & Morris, Norman. "Engrossment: the newborn's impact upon the father" in the *American Journal of Orthopsychiatry* 1974 **44**:520-31.

Hamilton, Marshall. *Father's Influence on Children*. Chicago: Nelson-Hall 1977.

Harrison, Fraser. *A Father's Diary*. London: Fontana 1985.

Hastings, James. *Dictionary of the Bible*. Second edition. Edinburgh: T. & T. Clark 1963.

Hearn, Jeff. *Birth and Afterbirth*. London: Achilles Heel, 7 St Mark's Rise, E8 2NJ, 1983.

Hearn, Jeff. "Childbirth, men and the problem of fatherhood" in *Radical Community Medicine* 1984 **17**:9-19.

Heider, Karl. "Dani sexuality: a low energy system" in *Man* (N.S.) 1976 **11**:188-201.

Hetherington, E.M. "Effects of father-absence on personality development in adolescent daughters" in *Developmental Psychology* 1972 **7**:313-26.

Hodson, Phillip. *Men*. London: Ariel Books 1984.

Holmberg, Allan. *Nomads of the Long Bow: The Sirionó of Eastern Bolivia*. Washington: Smithsonian Institution 1950 (reprinted, New York: Natural History Press, 1969).

House of Lords, The. *Parental Leave and Leave for Family Reasons*. Third report from the Select Committee on the European Communities. London: Her Majesty's Stationery Office 1985.

Ingham, Mary. *Men — The Male Myth Exposed*. London: Century 1984.

Jackson, Brian. *Fatherhood*. London: George, Allen & Unwin 1983.

Kay, Margarita (ed). *Anthropology of Human Birth*. Philadelphia: F.A. Davis 1982.

Kitzinger, Sheila. *Women as Mothers*. London: Fontana 1978.

Kitzinger, Sheila. *Woman's Experience of Sex*. London: Penguin 1985.

Kurtz, Zarina. "Medical and nursing staff attitudes to breastfeeding" in the *Journal of the Institute of Child Health* 1980 **18**(4).

Lamb, Michael (ed). *The Role of the Father in Child Development*. New York: Wiley 1975.

Leach, Edmund. *Political Systems of Highland Burma: A Study of Kachin Social Structure*. London: Bell & Son 1954.

Leach, Edmund. *Genesis as Myth*. London: Jonathan Cape 1969.

Levine, James. *Who Will Raise the Children?: New Options for Fathers (and Mothers)*. Philadelphia & New York: J.B. Lippincott 1976.

Lewis, Charlie. "'A feeling you can't scratch?': the effect of pregnancy and birth on married men" in Beail & McGuire (eds) 1982.

Lewis, Charlie. *Becoming a Father*. Milton Keynes & Philadelphia: Open University Press 1986.

Lewis, Charlie; Newson, Elizabeth & Newson, John. "Father participation through childhood and its relation to career aspirations and delinquency" in Beail & McGuire (eds) 1982.

Little, Peter. *The Baby Book for Dads*. London: New English Library 1980.

Lynn, David. *The Father: His Role in Child Development*. Monterey, California: Brooks/Cole 1974.

McKee, Lorna & O'Brien, Margaret (eds). *The Father Figure*. London: Tavistock Publications 1982.

Mainardi, Pat. "The politics of housework." New England Free Press, 60 Union Square, Somerville, Mass. 02143, 1968. Reprinted in Ellen Malos (ed) *The Politics of Housework*. London: Allison & Busby 1980.

Malinowski, Bronislaw. *The Father in Primitive Psychology*. London: Kegan Paul, Trench, Trubner & Co 1927.

Malinowski, Bronislaw. *The Sexual Life of Savages*. London: Routledge 1932.

Mandeville, Elizabeth. "Agnation, affinity and migration among the Kamano of the New Guinea Highlands" in *Man* (N.S.) 1979 **14**(1):105-23.

Masters, William & Johnson, Virginia. *Human Sexual Response*. Boston: Little, Brown 1966.

Mayle, Peter. *How to be a Pregnant Father*. London: Macmillan 1980.

Mead, Margaret. *The Family*. New York: Macmillan 1965.

Mead, Margaret. *Sex and Temperament in Three Primitive Societies*. New York & London: Routledge & Kegan Paul 1977.

Michaelson, Karen. *The Anthropology of Birth in America*. Bergin & Garvey 1986.

Miller, Warren & Newman, Lucile (eds). *The First Child and Family Formation*. Chapel Hill: Carolina Population Centre at University of North Carolina 1978.

Millett, Kate. *Sexual Politics*. New York: Avon Books 1970. London: Rupert Hart-Davis & Virago, 1977.

Mitscherlich, Alexander. *Society Without the Father*. London: Tavistock Publications 1969. New York: Schocken, 1970.

Money, John & Tucker, Patricia. *Sexual Signatures: On Being a Man or a Woman*. London: Harrap 1976.

Oakley, Ann. *Women Confined*. Oxford: Martin Robertson 1980.

Oates, Whitney & O'Neill, Eugene. *The Complete Greek Drama*. Volume 1. New York: Random House 1938.

Odent, Michel. Letter to *The Guardian* 10th August 1984.

Open University. *Getting Ready For Pregnancy*. Milton Keynes: Open University Press 1985.

Open University. *Understanding Pregnancy and Birth*. Milton Keynes: Open University Press 1985.

Owen, Ursula (ed). *Fathers: Reflections by Daughters*. London: Virago 1983.

Paige, Karen & Paige, Jeffrey. *The Politics of Reproductive Ritual*. Berkeley: University of California Press 1981.

Parke, Ross. *Fathering*. Glasgow: Fontana Paperbacks 1981.

Parsons, Betty. *The Expectant Father*. Kingswood, Surrey: Elliot Right Way Books 1984.

Pedersen, Frank (ed). *The Father-Infant Relationship*. New York: Praeger Publishers 1980.

Pedersen, Frank & Robson, Kenneth. "Father participation in infancy" in the *American Journal of Orthopsychiatry* 1969 **39**:466-72.

Peterson, G.H., Mehl, L.F., & Leiderman, P.H. "The role of some father-related variables in father attachment" in the *American Journal of Orthopsychiatry* 1975 49(2):330-8.

Phillips, Celeste & Anzalone, Joseph. *Fathering: Participation in Labor and Birth*. St Louis: C.V. Mosby 1978.

Quadnago, P.M. & Rockwell, J. "The effect of gonadal hormones in infancy on maternal behaviour in the adult rat" in *Hormones and Behaviour* 1972 **3**:55-62.

Radcliffe-Brown, A.R. *Structure and Function in Primitive Society*. London & Boston: Routledge & Kegan Paul 1952.

Rapoport, Rhona; Rapoport, Robert & Strelitz, Ziona. *Fathers, Mothers and Others: Towards New Alliances*. London & Boston: Routledge & Kegan Paul 1977.

Rebelsky, Freda & Hanks, Cheryl. "Fathers' verbal interactions with infants in the first three months of life" in *Child Development* 1971 **42**:63-8.

Renvoize, Jean. *Going Solo: Single Mothers by Choice*. London & Boston: Routledge & Kegan Paul 1985.

Rich, Adrienne. *Of Woman Born*. New York: Norton 1976. London: Virago, 1977.

Richards, M.; Dunn, J. & Antonis, B. "Caretaking in the first year of life: the role of father's and mother's isolation" in *Child: Care, Health and Development* 1975 **3**:23-36.

Richman, Joel. "Men's experiences of pregnancy and childbirth" in McKee & O'Brien (eds) 1982.

Roberts, David. "The paterfamilias of the Victorian governing classes" in Wohl 1978.

Roberts, Maureen. *Man Enough*. London: Chatto & Windus 1984.

Rorvik, David. *In His Image: The Cloning of a Man*. Philadelphia: Lippincott. London: Hamish Hamilton 1978.

Rosenthal, Kristine & Keshet, Harry. *Fathers Without Partners*. Totowa, New Jersey: Rowman & Littlefield 1981.

Ruskin, John. "Of queens' gardens" in *Sesame and Lilies*. London 1865, Chicago: Homewood, 1902.

Russell, Graeme. *The Changing Role of Fathers*. Milton Keynes: Open University Press 1983.

Salzman, Philip. "Ideology and change in Middle Eastern tribal societies" in *Man* (N.S.) 1978 **13**:618-37.

Sargant, William. *Battle for the Mind*. London: William Heinemann 1957.

Schwimmer, Erik. "Virgin birth" in *Man* (N.S.) 1969 **4**:132-3.

Seel, Richard. "It's only natural?" in *New Generation* 1983 **2**(3):9

Seel, Richard. *Becoming a Father*. London: National Childbirth Trust, 9 Queensborough Terrace, W2 3TB, 1984.

Seel, Richard. "Birth rite: a possible link between obstetric practice and postnatal depression" in *Health Visitor* 1986 **59**(6):182-4.

Schaefer, George. *The Expectant Father*. New York: Barnes & Noble 1972.

Smiles, Samuel. *Character*. London: Murray 1882.

Snowden, Robert & Mitchell, Duncan. *The Artificial Family*. London: George Allen & Unwin 1981.

Stafford, Linley. *One Man's Family: A Single Father and his Children*. New York: Random House 1978.

Steinberg, David. *Fatherjournal*. New York: Times Change Press, 62 W.14th Street, NY10011, 1977.

Stolz, Lois. *Father Relations of War-Born Children*. Stanford: University Press 1954. (Reprinted, New York: Greenwood Press 1968.)

Strathern, Andrew. "Kinship, descent and locality: some New Guinea examples" in Goody (ed) 1973.

Sundin, Ju Ju. "Preparing father for birth" in *Childbirth Educator* August 1985.

Trimmer, Eric. *You're a Father!* London: Pagoda Books 1983.

Turner, Victor. *The Ritual Process*. Chicago: Aldine, London: Routledge & Kegan Paul 1969.

Valentine, Alan (ed). *Fathers to Sons: Advice Without Consent*. Norman, Oklahoma: University Press 1963.

Vilar, Esther. *The Manipulated Man*. London: Abelard-Schuman 1972.

Ward, Elizabeth. *Father-Daughter Rape*. London: The Women's Press 1984.

Welburn, Vivien. *Postnatal Depression*. London: Fontana 1980.

Whittingham, D.G. "Parthenogenesis in mammals" in C.A. Finn (ed) *Oxford Reviews of Reproductive Biology, Volume 2*. Oxford: Clarendon Press 1980.

Wohl, Anthony (ed). *The Victorian Family*. London: Croon Helm 1978.

Woollett, Anne; White, David & Lyon, Louise. "Observations of fathers at birth" in Beail & McGuire 1982.

Wynn, Margaret. *Fatherless Families*. London: Michael Joseph 1964.

Index

Men and Friendship by Stuart Miller

This remarkable book has been praised everywhere for its boldness, sensitivity, and courage. Stuart Miller examines the sorry state of friendship between men today, most of them busy with marriage and careers. He shows that most men have close friendships in youth but lose them later. Though many would like an adult version of the old comradeship and intimacy, social conditions make real friendship hard to come by. But close friendship can embolden men, making the hero in every man much closer to realization. A true friendship can make men stronger, wiser, and so women say, better lovers! By detailing the difficulties and suggesting solutions, Miller opens practical and poetic possibilities. It is time to revive the great tradition of male friendship - the deep, serious, and generous kind - and *Men and Friendship* points the way.

Dr. Stuart Miller has been a psychology editor, English professor, and was founder-president of the Institute for the Study of Humanistic Medicine.

The critics say:

USA

"Miller has a fine talent for capturing the vicissitudes of human relation-ships from the inside, and his book is an invitation for men to re-examine the hole in their lives where real friendship could be." *Boston Globe*

"A profoundly personal and deeply engaging meditation on 'the necessity for an art of male friendship' ... A heartening document." *Assoc. Humanistic Psychology Newsletter*

"Miller's insights ... reveal a keen intellect deeply engaged. His objection to the shallow facade that passes for friendship is well taken." *Best Sellers*

Britain

"Miller was encouraged by Rollo May, who told him 'we are alone, we have lost our myths, we are anxious about death, so we need people to stand by us. To create a new myth about male friendship would help'. Judging by the emotional response from a number of readers, he may have succeeded." *The Guardian*

"An excellent book, a lovely book, a true book of love." *New Statesman*

Canada

"A wise book ... You can't help but admire him ... his book reminds us of the mystery and unpredictability of friendship." *Newsday*

France

"A sensitive work, courageously honest and sincere; no one can remain indifferent to the theme of this book." *Radio France*

"A remarkable sociological analysis, a fascinating book." *Cosmopolitan*

Italy

"A book which with great sensitivity and subtlety dares to enter a hidden shadowy zone of our contemporary live ... it helps us rediscover an essential element of our emotional nature." *La Nazione*

Holland

"The book is essential, for all men and women." *Telegraaf*

198 x 216mm, 224pp   ISBN 946551 02 2   Paper £4.95 (US $7.95)

Finding a Way, a Realist's Guide to Self-Help Therapy
by Alex Howard

This original work is designed for those for whom spiritual values are important yet who feel that neither the Church nor conventional psychology quite answer the individual's needs for self-discovery and relating to others.

It is a teach yourself course, going through the vital areas of living where so often we have learned to accept second best. So we say; "I don't want to commit myself" or "I can't make any difference". Can we learn to relax, to be better listeners, to be more assertive, to avoid useless worry and self-torture, to co-operate, to take responsibility, to be more effective parents?

Though none of these skills in human relationship are easy to master, a practical programme is presented, with questions for self-assessment at every stage.

Alex Howard teaches a variety of courses in practical psychology for the general public, and is tutor-organiser for the Workers' Educational Association on Tyneside.

"This exceptionally helpful and down to earth book is a revealing, teach yourself course in removing those masks we hide behind." *Science of Thought Review*

216 x 135 mm, 224pp   ISBN 946551 13 8   Paper £4.95 (US $8.95)

For a full catalogue please write to:

Gateway Books, 19 Circus Place, Bath, BA1 2PW, or to
Slawson Communications, 3719 Sixth Ave., San Diego CA 92103

(Note: prices subject to change)